BOOKBINDING

A Guide
to the Literature

BOOKBINDING

A Guide to the Literature

Compiled by *Vito J. Brenni*

GREENWOOD PRESS
Westport, Connecticut • London, England

Library of Congress Cataloging in Publication Data

Brenni, Vito Joseph, 1923-
  Bookbinding.

  Includes indexes.
  1. Bookbinding—Bibliography. I. Title.
Z266.5.B73 1982   016.6863   82-15810
ISBN 0-313-23718-2 (lib. bdg.)

Library of Congress Catalog Card Number: 82-15810
ISBN: 0-313-23718-2

First published in 1982

Greenwood Press
A division of Congressional Information Service, Inc.
88 Post Road West, Westport, Connecticut 06881

Printed in the United States of America

10 9 8 7 6 5 4 3 2 1

CONTENTS

PREFACE

I have compiled this bibliography on bookbinding because I believe that every subject needs a guide to the literature. Earlier bibliographies on the subject, useful as they are, were not designed to be guides to the literature in the way in which I have prepared this one. I have classified the literature under many headings, and I have provided a detailed subject index as well as a separate author index. I have tried to be comprehensive, though not exhaustive. Along with the literature of bookbinding, I have included publications on book jackets because they cover the binding, and bookplates because they are attached to the binding. The "List of Binders, Binding Designers, and Binding Decorators" near the end of the volume is the only compilation, so far as I know, that includes binders of all periods and for many countries.

For this bibliography, bookbinding is defined as anything that covers the pages of the codex book, or the form of the book with which most of us are familiar. Bindings or covers for clay tablets, papyrus rolls, the microform book, and other forms of the book are not included, except in some of the general readings. The time span is the early Christian period to the present. The more than 1,500 publications cited include books, theses, sales and exhibit catalogs, periodical articles, and essays in books. The publications are in English, French, German, Spanish, Italian, and many other languages. Except for the Bible, no publications about the bindings of individual books are included.

The bibliography begins with reference works and continues with such topics as bookbinding design and methods, materials, machines and tools, decoration, a chronological history, history by individual country, the care and repair of bindings, the study of bookbinding, audiovisual aids, bookplates, and book jackets. Reference works include bibliographies that may be consulted for publications not listed in this guide. The chapter on decoration has separate lists of publications on book edges and endpapers. The longest chapter in the bibliography has entries for the history of bookbinding in more than thirty countries. Included with the countries, in alphabetical order, are sections for "Hebrew" and "Islam." Particular attention has been given to those countries that have made the greatest contribution to the art of bookbinding, among them France, Great Britain, and Germany. For these and several other countries a special effort was made to cover the twentieth century and the contemporary scene. The chapters on bookplates and book jackets also have sections for individual countries.

Included among the citations are books and articles about individual binders and book collectors. In addition, many other entries are annotated to indicate that illustrations of the work of particular binders are included. Other annotations provide information about editions, special features, contents, people and places, and book reviews. Bibliographies, glossaries, and lists of binders are among the special features of the works noted.

Checklists of titles are included for libraries that may want to improve their collections on bookbinding. Some of the large university and college libraries may want to buy all of them, while the smaller ones may want to be more selective. The list for the medium-sized public library was compiled for the city with a population of 200,000 to 500,000. Libraries in larger cities may want to use the list for the university library.

Following the library checklists is an alphabetical list of some 550 binders, which complements the bibliography by providing brief biographical information and adds many more names of binders, binding designers, and binding decorators to those in the bibliography.

Finally, there is a short list of book collectors who gave special attention to fine bindings.

The short glossary was compiled to help the reader understand some of the terms in the titles included in the bibliography. For other terms the dictionaries listed in the reference chapter should be consulted. *Glaister's Glossary of the Book* (2d ed., 1979) is one of the best. A good list of French binding terms is included in Roger Fourny's *Manuel de Reliure* (2d ed., 1965).

The author index is complete for authors and editors only. When a publication has a corporate and a personal author, both names are included. Translators and revisers are omitted.

The subject index attempts to provide access to all the titles and all the information in the notes, including the names of many binders, binding designers, decorators, and book collectors. Many "see also" references follow the entries for countries, referring the reader to entries for smaller geographic areas such as cities and provinces.

For the author of a book the best part of the preface is the acknowledgment, because he remembers all those people who provided help along the long journey of research. Without them the author may never have reached his destination. It is, therefore, with gratitude and pleasure that I acknowledge the help of the many librarians at the University of Michigan and Michigan State University, where I did most of the work on this book.

BOOKBINDING

A Guide to the Literature

1

REFERENCE WORKS

Bibliographies

1. Amelung, Peter. "Einbandforschung 1966-1971; eine Literaturbericht." Gutenberg Jahrbuch 1972, p.373-409.

2. _____. "Einbandforschung 1972-1976; eine Literaturbericht. Teil II." Gutenberg Jahrbuch 1978, p.313-42.

3. Bogeng, Gustav A. Die grossen Bibliophilen: Geschichte der Bücher-sammler und ihrer Sammlungen. Leipzig, Seemann, 1922. 3 vols. plates. facs.

   Volume 3 contains a long bibliography (284p).

4. Grolier Club, N.Y. List of books and articles relating to bookbind-ing found in the library. N.Y., 1907. 117-84 p.

5. Gruel, Léon. Manuel historique et bibliographique de l'amateur de reliures. Paris, Gruel and Engelmann, 1887-1905. 2 vols. illus. plates. facs.

6. Helwig, Hellmuth. Handbuch der Einbandkunde. Hamburg, Maximilian-Gesellschaft, 1953-55. 2 vols. illus. plates. Registerband. Namen-und Ortsregister zur Biobibliographie der Buchbinder Europas bis etwa 1850. Hamburg, Maximilian-Gesellschaft, 1955. 159p.

   Vol. I contains essays on individual topics followed by long bibli-ographies. The 2d vol. is a biobibliography of European binders up to about 1850. The third volume contains lists of binders by place.

7. Herbst, Hermann. Bibliographie der Buchbinderei-Literatur, 1924-32. Leipzig, Hiersemann, 1933. 169p.

8. _____. "Bucheinbandliteratur 1933-1937." Jahrbuch der Einband-kunst 4:189-215, 1937.

9. Hobson, Anthony. The literature of bookbinding. London, Published for the National Book League by the Cambridge Univ. Press, 1954. 15p.

10. Hobson, Geoffrey D. "Books on bookbinding." Book collectors quarterly no. 7:70-84. 1932.

11. Mejer, Wolfgang. Bibliographie der Buchbinderei-Literatur. Leipzig, Hiersemann, 1925. 208p.

12. Needham, Paul. Twelve centuries of bookbindings 400-1600. N.Y., Pierpont Morgan Library, Oxford Univ. Press, 1979. 338p. 100 plates

     Contains an excellent list of titles on bookbinding, p.311-23.

13. Nelson, Charles A. Catalogue raisonnée; works on bookbinding practical and historical, examples of bookbindings from the collection of S. P. Avery, exhibited at Columbia Univ. Library, N.Y., Priv. printed, 1903. 136p.

14. Pratt Institute Free Library. "Bibliography of articles containing illustrations of bookbindings to be found in books and periodicals in the Pratt Institute Library." Pratt Institute monthly 7:207-16. 1899.

15. Prideaux, Sarah T. "A bibliography of bookbinding." Library 4:15-24, 50-56, 90-95. 1892.

16. Schmidt-Künsemüller, Friedrich A. "20 Jahre Einbandkunst." Archiv für Geschichte des Buchwesens 18: columns 1097-1144. 1967.

17. _____. "Weitere 10 Jahre Einbandforschung." Archiv für Geschichte des Buchwesens 18: columns 731-98. 1977.

Dictionaries and Encyclopedias

18. Birkenmajer, Aleksander et al., eds. Encyklopedia wiedzy o ksiaze. Wroclaw, 1971. 2874 columns. illus.

19. Diehl, Edith. "Glossary." (In her Bookbinding, its background and technique. N.Y., Rinehart, 1946. vol. 1, p.223-34)

20. Glaister, Geoffrey A. Glaister's glossary of the book. 2nd ed., completely revised. Berkeley, Univ. of California Press, 1979. 551p. illus.

21. Haller, Margaret. The book collector's fact book. N.Y., Arco, 1976. 271p.

22. Harrod, Leonard M. The librarians' glossary. 4th rev. ed. London, Deutsch, 1977. 903p.

23. Kersten, Paul. Die Verzierungstechniken des Bucheinbändes. 2d ed. Halle, Knapp, 1939. 31p.

24. Kuhn, Hilde. Wörterbuch der Handbuchbinderei und der Restaurierung von Einbänden, Papyri, Handschriften, Graphiken, Autographen, Urkunden und Globen in deutscher, englischer, französischer und italienischer Sprache. Stuttgart, Hettler, 1969. 66p.

25. Lexikon des Buchwesens. Hrsg. von Joachim Kirchner. Stuttgart,
Hiersemann, 1952-56. 4 vols. illus.

26. Nordisk Leksikon for bogvaesen. Redg. af E. Dansten et al. Copenhagen, 1949-62. 2 vols.

27. Peddie, Robert A. "Publishers' bindings, 1762-1850; a list of
terms." Library world 46:20-21, Aug.-Sept. 1943.

28. Peters, Jean, ed. The bookman's glossary. 5th ed. N.Y., Bowker,
1975. 169p.

29. Zaehnsdorf, Joseph W. "Glossary of the technical terms and imple-
ments used in bookbinding." (In The art of bookbinding. London, Bell,
1879. p.167-78)

30. _____. A short history of bookbinding and a glossary of styles
and terms used in bookbinding. London, Zaehnsdorf, 1895. 32p.

2

BOOKBINDING DESIGN, METHODS, AND OTHER WRITINGS ON TECHNIQUE

Design

31. Bradley, William A. "Elements of design in book covers."
Printing art 12:363-69, Feb. 1909.

32. Jennett, Seán. "Binding design." (In The making of books. N.Y.,
Pantheon, 1951. p.411-28)

33. Prideaux, Sarah T. "Design in bookbinding." (In Bookbinders and
their craft. London, Zaehnsdorf, 1903. p.79-108)

34. Williamson, Hugh. "Bookbinding." (In Methods of book design.
London, Oxford Univ. Press, 1966. p.312-40)

Technique

English Language Publications--19th Century

35. "The art of bookbinding; an interview with Mr. Cobden-Sanderson."
Studio 2:53-56, Nov. 1893.

36. The bookbinder's manual. London, Cowie and Strange, 1829? 124p.
4th ed., 1832.

  Attributed to George Cowie, a printer.

37. Crane, J. Eden. Bookbinding for amateurs; being descriptions of the
various tools and appliances required and minute instructions for their
effective use. London, Upcott Gill, 1885. 184p. illus.

38. Hannett, John. Bibliopegia, or the art of bookbinding in all its
branches. London, Groombridge, 1835. 212p. plates. 4th ed., 1848.
6th ed., 1865.

  The author's name is sometimes given as John Andrews Arnett.

39. Nicholson, James B. A manual on the art of bookbinding, containing
full instructions in the different branches of forwarding, gilding, and
finishing. Phila., Baird, 1856. 318p. illus. plates.

40. Parry, Henry. The art of bookbinding... London, Baldwin, Cradock
and Joy, 1818. 92p.

41. Tomlinson, Charles, ed. "Bookbinding." (In Cyclopedia of useful arts... London, G. Virtue, 1854. vol. 1, p. 152-62)

42. Zaehnsdorf, Joseph W. The art of bookbinding. London, Bell, 1879. 187p. illus.

English Language Publications--20th Century

43. Banister, Manly M. Bookbinding as a handcraft. N.Y., Sterling, 1975. 160p. illus.

44. _____. Pictorial manual of bookbinding. N.Y., Ronald Press, 1958. 40p. illus.

45. Burdett, Eric. The craft of bookbinding. Newton Abbot, David and Charles, 1975. 400p. illus.

46. Clough, Eric A. Bookbinding for librarians. London, Association of Assistant Librarians, 1957. 204p. illus.

47. Cockerell, Douglas. Bookbinding and the care of books. 5th ed. London, Pitman, 1953. 345p. plates.

48. _____. A note on bookbinding. London, W. H. Smith, 1904. 26p.

49. _____. Some notes on bookbinding. London, Oxford Univ. Press, 1925. 105p. illus.

50. Darley, Lionel S. Introduction to bookbinding. London, Faber and Faber, 1965. 118p. illus.

51. Diehl, Edith. Bookbinding, its background and technique. N.Y., Rinehart, 1946. 2 vols. illus.

52. Feipel, Louis and Browning, Earl. Library binding manual, prepared under the direction of the Joint Committee of the American Library Association and the Library Binding Institute. Chicago, American Library Association, 1951. 74p. illus.

53. Franck, Peter. A lost link in the technique of hand bookbinding and how I found it. Gaylordsville, Conn., Printed at the Hawthorne House, 1941. 18p. illus.

54. Hasluck, Paul N., ed. Bookbinding with numerous engravings and diagrams. London, Cassell, 1902. 160p. illus.

    Includes a chapter on marbling and staining of papers.

55. Hewitt-Bates, James S. Bookbinding. 8th ed. Leicester, Dryad Press, 1967. 127p. illus.

56. Johnson, Arthur W. The Thames and Hudson manual of bookbinding. London, Thames and Hudson, 1981. 224p. illus.

57. Johnson, Pauline. Creative bookbinding. Seattle, Univ. of Washington Press, 1964. 263p. illus.

58. Kay, Jabez. Advanced bookbinding. London, Cassell, 1932. 72p.

59. Lewis, Arthur W. Basic bookbinding. N.Y., Dover, 1957. 144p. illus.

60. Library Binding Institute, Boston. Library binding handbook. Boston, 1963. 49p.

61. Lydenberg, Harry M. and Archer, John. The care and repair of books. Rev. by John Alden. 4th rev. ed. N.Y., Bowker, 1960. 122p.

62. Perry, Kenneth F. and Baab, Clarence T. The binding of books. rev. ed. Bloomington, McKnight and McKnight, 1967. 190p. illus.

63. Pleger, John J. Bookbinding and its auxiliary branches. Chicago, Inland Printer Co., 1914. 4 vols. illus. plates.

64. Stephen, George A. Commercial bookbinding; a description of the various processes and the various machines used. London, Stonhill, 1910. 59p. 70 illus. and diagrams.

65. Tauber, Maurice F., ed. Library binding manual; a handbook of useful procedures for the maintenance of library volumes. Boston, Library Binding Institute, 1972. 185p.

66. Town, Laurence. Bookbinding by hand, for students and craftsmen. 2d ed. London, Faber and Faber, 1963. 207p. illus.

67. U.S. Government Printing Office. Theory and practice of bookbinding. rev. ed. Wash., D.C., 1962. 244p.

68. Vaughan, Alexander J. Modern bookbinding. Leicester, Rathby, Lawrence, 1946. 218p. illus.

69. Watson, Aldren A. Hand bookbinding; a manual of instruction. N.Y., Bell, 1963. 93p. illus.

Foreign Language Publications--18th and 19th Centuries

70. Adam, Paul. Die praktischen Arbeiten des Buchbinders. Vienna, Hartleben, 1898. 128p.

     Translated in 1903 by Thomas E. Maw and published by Scott, Greenwood in London.

71. Bosquet, Emile. Traité théorique et pratique de l'art du relieur. Paris, Baudry, 1890. 323p. illus.

72. Gauffecourt, Jean-Vincent Capronnier de. Traité de la reliure des livres. La Motte, 1763. 72p.

     First printed work in French devoted to bookbinding. The author lived in Geneva and Lyon.

73. Le Normand, Louis. Manual del encuadernador. Barcelona, 1846. 334p. illus.

74. _____. Manuel du relieur dans toutes ses parties. Paris, Roret, 1827. 344p. plates.

75. _____. Nouveau manuel complet du relieur en tous genres. Nouvelle édition refondue et augmentée par M. Maigne. Paris, Roret, 1879. 424p. illus.

76. Schaefer, L. Vollständiges Handbuch der Buchbindekunst. Quedlinburg, Basse, 1845. 139p. plates.

Foreign Language Publications--20th Century

77. Berger, Leopoldo. Manual practice e illustrado do encadernador. Rio de Janeiro, Livravia AGIR, 1946. 135p. illus.

78. Bosquet, Emile. Guide manuel théorique et pratique de l'ouvrier ou practicien-relieur. Paris, 1903. 308p. 65 illus.

79. Brugalla, Emilio. Tres ensayos sobre el arte de la encuadernación. Barcelona, Associacion de Bibliofilos de Barcelona, 1954. 91p. plates.

80. Colombo, Pio. Il legatore di libri. Turin, Libreria Editrice Internationale, 1913-14. 2 vols.

81. Giannini, Giulio G. Il dilletante legatore di libri. Milan, 1908. 204p. illus. 6th ed., 1951. illus. plates.

82. Henningsen, Thorwald. Das Handbuch für den Buchbinder. 2d ed. St. Gallen, Hostettler, 1969. 468p. illus.

83. Ikegami, Kojiro. Hon no tsukurikata. 1979.

84. Le Bailly, Arlette. Initiation à la reliure d'art. Paris, Bornemann, 1971. 56p. illus. plates.

85. Lemoine, Simone. Manuel pratique du relieur. Paris, Larousse, 1953. 268p. illus.

86. Lueers, Heinrich. Das Fachwissen des Buchbinders. 2d ed. Stuttgart, Hettler, 1941. 396p. illus. 4th ed., 1944.

87. Musarra, Aldo. Para aprender encuadernación. Buenos Aires, Editorial Hobby, 1946. 173p. illus.

88. Pay, Sigrid. Haandbok for amatoer-bokbindare. Kristiana, Norsk Naeringsliv, 1919. 74p. illus.

89. Rhein, Adolf. Das Buchbinderbuch. Halle, Knapp, 1954. 401p.

90. Roux, Charles. Pour le relieur. 2d ed. Paris, 1931. 181p.

91. Tonegato, Elio. <u>Rilegare per hobby</u>. Milan, Hoepli, 1970. 141p. illus. plates.

92. Wiese, Fritz. <u>Der Bucheinband</u>. 3d ed. Stuttgart, 1953. 408p. 4th ed., 1964.

93. Wolf-Lefranc, Madeleine and Vermuyse, Charles. <u>La reliure</u>. Paris, Bailliere, 1957. 344p. illus.

3

MATERIALS

General Works

94.   Clough, Eric. A. "The raw materials of bookbinding: cloth, leather, leather cloth." (In Bookbinding for librarians. London, Association of Assistant Librarians, 1957. p.26-38)

95.   Gorenflo, Edward, firm, N.Y. Specimen Book. N.Y., 1885. 16p. illus.

96.   Nitz, Hermann. Die Materialen für Buch und Bucheinband und ihre sachgemässe Verarbeitung. 2d ed. Halle, Knapp, 1950. 157p. illus. 3d ed., 1953.

97.   Thuma, Max. Die Werkstoffe des Buchbinders, ihre Herstellung und Verarbeitung. 3d ed. Stuttgart, 1949. 87p.

98.   Victoria and Albert Museum, South Kensington. National Art Library. Notes on printing and bookbinding; a guide to the exhibition of tools and materials in the processes. By S. T. Prideaux. London, 1921. 40p. 16 plates.

Cloth

99.   Antrobus, Mary S. and Preece, Louisa. Needlework through the ages. London, Hodder and Stoughton, 1928. 413p. illus. plates.

      See embroidered bindings on pages 206, 287, 339, 233, 260-61, and plates 70 and 94.

100.   Carter, John. "Notes on the early years of cloth binding." Book collectors quarterly 6:46-56, Apr.-June 1952.

101.   _____. "Origins of publishers' cloth binding." Colophon 2, part 8, 1931. (unpaged; about 10 pages in length)

102.   Davenport, Cyril. "Bindings in velvet." Book lover's magazine 8:126-31. 1908.

103.   Hartzog, Martha. "Nineteenth-century cloth bindings." Publications of the Bibliographical Society of America 61:114-19, second quarter 1967.

104.   Leighton, Douglas. "Canvas and book-cloth; an essay in beginnings." Library 3:39-49, June 1948.

105. Sadleir, Michael. "The nomenclature of nineteenth-century cloth grains." Book collector 2:54-58, spring 1953.

Taken from Sadleir's XIX century fiction (London, Constable, 1951. 2 vols.)

106. Shaw, Harold E. "Book cloths." (In Hitchcock, Frederick H., ed. The building of a book. 2d ed. N.Y., Bowker, 1929. p.198-204)

107. Tanselle, G. Thomas. "The specification of binding cloth." Library 5:246-47, Sept. 1966.

Ivory

108. Cust, A. M. The ivory workers of the Middle Ages. London, Bell, 1902. 170p. illus.

See p.10, 25, 26, 52-57. Contains 3 illustrations of ivory covers.

109. Longhurst, Margaret H. and Morey, Charles R. "The covers of the Lorsch Gospels: I. The Vatican cover." Speculum 3:64-74, Jan. 1928.

110. Paris. Bibliothèque Nationale. "Reliures d'ivoire et d'orfèvrerie (1x -xiv)." (In Les plus belles reliures de la réunion des bibliothèques nationales. Paris, Van Oest, 1929. p.1-5)

111. Sotheran, firm, booksellers, London. Illustrated supplement to catalog 819: beautiful Cosway bindings in the finest Levant morocco... with miniatures on ivory by Miss Currie. London, 1930? 31p. illus.

112. Wixom, William D. "Ottonian ivory book cover." Cleveland Museum bulletin 55:273-89, Nov. 1968.

Leather

113. Bookbinder's manual, containing a full description of leather and vellum binding... 4th ed. London, 1832. 124p.

Attributed to George Cowie.

114. Elliott, Roy G. "Leather as a bookbinding material." Designer Bookbinders review 2:2-8, autumn 1973; 3:11-16, spring 1974; 4:11-15, autumn 1974.

115. Forbes, R. J. "Leather in antiquity." (In Studies in ancient technology. Leiden, Brill, 1966. vol. 5, p. 1-79)

116. Goldschmidt, Ernst P. "Some cuir-cisele bookbindings in English libraries." Library 13:337-65, Mar. 1933.

117. Moore, Frederick N. The art of making leather for books. Boston, 1927? 16p.

118. O'Flaherty, Fred et al., eds. The chemistry and technology of leather. N.Y., Reinhold, 1956-65. 4 vols.

119. Récy, Georges de. The decoration of leather. From the French by Maude Nathan. London, Constable, 1905. 104p.

120. Reed, Ronald. Ancient skins, parchments and leathers. London, Seminar Press, 1972. 331p. illus.

121. Report of the Committee on Leather for Bookbinding. Ed. for the Society of Arts and the Worshipful Company of Leathersellers by Viscount Cobham and Henry T. Wood. London, Bell, 1905. 93p. illus.

122. Smith, Philip. "Building images with leather." (In New directions in bookbinding. London, Studio Vista, 1974. p.48-51)

123. _____. "Leather." (In New directions in bookbinding. London, Studio Vista, 1974. p.42-48)

124. _____. "Manufacture of leather." (In New directions in book-binding. London, Studio Vista, 1974. p.194-96)

125. _____. "Puckered leather." (In New directions in bookbinding. London, Studio Vista, 1974. p.60-63)

126. Warner, John. "Modern bookbinding leathers." Library Association record 7;153-64, Sept. 1929.

127. Waterer, John W. "Leather." (In Singer, Charles et al., eds. A history of technology. Oxford, Clarendon Press, 1956. vol. 2, p.147-87)

128. Wilson, John A. Modern practice in leather manufacture. N.Y., Reinhold, 1941. 744p. illus.

Metal

129. Bunt, Cyril G. "Treasured books in silver livery." Connoisseur 114:71-77, Dec. 1944.

130. Grolier Club, N.Y. Exhibition of silver, embroidered, and curious bookbindings...the Grolier Club of the city of New York, April 16 to May 9, 1903. N.Y., 1903. 86p.

131. Hayward, J. F. "Silver bindings from the Abbey collection." Connoisseur 130:98-104, Oct. 1952.

132. Jones, E. Alfred. "Two Charles I silver bindings at Cambridge." Burlington magazine 79:129, Oct. 1941.

133. "List of manuscripts and examples of metal and ivory bindings from the Bibliotheca Lindesiana. Exhibited to the Bibliographical Society, at the Grafton Galleries, 13th June 1898." Trans. of the Bibliographical Society, 1898, p. 213-32.

> Gives 3 examples with brief description. Enamel bindings are included.

134. Prideaux, Sarah T. "The metal ornament of bound books." Magazine of art 14:316-21, July 1891.

> Reprinted in her An historical sketch of bookbinding (1893), p.169-99.

Paper

Technology

135. Britt, Kenneth W., ed. Handbook of pulp and paper technology. N.Y., Reinhold, 1964. 537p. 2d ed., 1970.

136. Clapperton, Robert H. Modern papermaking. 2d ed. Oxford, Blackwell, 1941. 376p. 3d ed., 1952.

137. Higham, Robert R. A handbook of paper making. London, Oxford Univ. Press, 1963. 294p.

138. La Lande, Joseph-Jérôme. Art de faire le papier. Paris, Saillant et Nyon, 1761. 150p. plates, nouvelle édition, 1820.

139. Le Normand, Louis S. Manuel du fabricant de papiers, ou de l'art de la papeterie. Paris, Roret, 1833. 2 vols. and atlas.

140. Mierziński, Stanislaus. Handbuch der praktischen Papier-fabrikation. Vienna, 1886. 3 vols.

141. Witham, George S. Modern pulp and paper making. 2d ed. N.Y., Reinhold, 1942. 705p. 3d ed., rev. and ed. by John B. Calkin in 1957.

History

142. Blum, André. Les origines du papier, de l'imprimerie et de la gravure; illustrées de 80 gravures. Paris, Editions de la Tournelle, 1935. 252p.

143. Bockwitz, Hans H. Papiermacher und Buchdrucker im Zeitalter Gutenbergs. Zittau, 1939. 18p.

144. Hunter, Dard. "Fifteenth century papermaking." Ars typographica 3:37-51, July 1926.

145. _____. Papermaking; the history and technique of an ancient craft. 2d ed. London, Knopf, 1947. 611p. and xxxviip. of index.

146. Hunter, Dard. "The story of paper." Natural history magazine
40:577-97, Oct. 1937.

147. Kent, Norman. "A brief history of papermaking." American artist
31:36-41, Oct. 1967.

148. Latour, A. "Paper, a historical outline." Ciba review 6:2630-39,
Feb. 1949.

149. Overton, John. "A note on technical advances in the manufacture
of paper before the nineteenth century." (In Singer, Charles et al., eds.
A History of technology. Oxford, Clarendon Press, 1957. vol. 3, p.411-16)

Parchment and Vellum

150. Bookbinder's manual, containing a full description of leather and
vellum binding... 4th ed. London, 1832. 124p.

     Attributed to George Cowie.

151. Johnson, Richard R. "The role of parchment in Greco-Roman
antiquity." Ph.D. dissertation, Univ. of California at Los Angeles,
1968. 152p.

152. Lüthi-Tschanz, Karl J. Das Pergament: seine Geschichte, seine
Anwendung. Bern, Büchler, 1938. 34p.

153. Reed, Ronald. Ancient skins, parchments and leathers. London,
Seminar Press, 1972. 331p. illus.

154. _____. The nature and making of parchment. Leeds, Elmete Press,
1975. 99p.

155. Saxl, Hedwig. "Histology of parchment." Technical studies in the
field of fine arts 8:3-9, July 1939.

156. _____. "A note on parchment." (In Singer, Charles et al., eds.
A history of technology. Oxford, Clarendon Press, 1956. vol. 2,
p.187-90)

157. Thompson, Daniel V. "Medieval parchment-making." Library
16:113-17, June 1935.

Other Materials

158. Fizelière, Albert-André de la. Des émaux cloisonnés et de leur
introduction dans la reliure des livres. Paris, Aubry, 1870. 16p.

159. Furler, Alfred. Technologie der Klebebindung: Materialen, Klebstoffe, Productionsmittel. Stuttgart, Verlag Deutscher Drucker, 1971.
306p. 272 illus. and graphs.

160. Graham, Rigby. "Bookbinding with human skin." Private library 6:14-18, Jan. 1965.

161. Rupp, Emil. Die Klebstoffe für Buchbinderei und Papierverarbeitung. Halle, Knapp, 1951. 137p. illus.

162. Thompson, Lawrence S. "Bibliopegia fantastica." New York Public Library bulletin 51:71-90, Feb. 1947.

163. _____. "Tanned human skin." Medical Library Association bulletin 34:93-102, Apr. 1946.

164. Verdier, Philippe. "Emaux mosans et rhéno-mosans dans les collections des Etats-Unis." Revue belge d'archéologie et d'histoire de l'art 44:3-84. 1975.

        Contains illustrations of enamel plaques on bindings, p.47-55.

4

BINDING MACHINERY
AND TOOLS

165. Belozerskii, Leonid K. <u>Broshnurovochno-perepletnye mashiny</u>. Moscow, 1960. 551p. illus.

166. Crane, J. Eden. <u>Bookbinding for amateurs; being descriptions of the various tools and appliances required and minute instructions for their effective use</u>. London, Upcott Gill, 1885. 184p. illus.

167. "Encuadernación." <u>Enciclopedia universal ilustrada</u> 19:1197-1216.

   Contains many illustrations of binding machines.

168. Gaskill and Copper, firm, Phila. <u>Patterns of rolls, stamps, scrolls, and connecting lines for ornamenting the covers of books</u>. Phila., 1847. 1p. 24 plates.

   This Phila. company was the source of much of the ornamentation used on the bindings of American gift books and annuals during the 19th century.

169. Hobson, Geoffrey D. "Some early bindings and binders' tools." <u>Library</u> 19:202-49, Sept. 1938.

170. Hobson, Kenneth. "Some notes on the history and development of bookbinders' stamps and tools." <u>Print</u> 8:37-42, Dec. 1953.

171. Hoe, firm, N.Y. <u>Catalog of binders' presses and materials</u>. N.Y., 1881. 172p. illus.

172. Meier, Henry. "The presses of the bookbinder." <u>Print collector's quarterly</u> 28:25-31, Feb. 1941.

173. Sanborn, George H. and Sons. <u>Sanborn's paper cutting machines and bookbinders' machinery</u>. N.Y., 1891. 56p. illus.

174. Stephen, George A. <u>Commercial bookbinding; a description of the processes and the various machines used</u>. London, Stonhill, 1910. 59p. 70 illus. and diagrams.

175. Sterne, Harold E. <u>Catalogue of nineteenth century bindery equipment</u>. Cincinnati, Ye Olde Printery, 1979. 272p. illus.

176. Toronto University. Library. Dept. of Rare Books and Collections. <u>The Birdsall collection of bookbinders' finishing tools</u>. By Emrys Evans and Rachel Grover. Toronto, 1972. 22p. 10 illus.

5

DECORATION

(For stamped bindings see individual countries.)

General Works

177. Art and design in the decoration of bookbindings. A collection of valuable and interesting books in beautiful and appropriate covers. c.1910. 117p. illus.

178. Bonet, Paul. "Decoration of bindings." Craft horizons 10:15-17, summer 1950.

179. Cardenal, De. "Evolution générale de la décoration de la couverture du livre." Bulletin du bibliophile 17:345-57. 1938.

180. Cartier, Alfred. De la décoration extérieure des livres et de l'histoire de la reliure depuis le 15ᵃ siècle. Geneva, Impr. Ch. Schuchardt, 1885. 54p. 12 plates.

181. Cundall, Joseph. On ornamental art applied to ancient and modern bookbinding. Illustrated with specimens of various dates and countries. London, At the House of the Society of Arts, 1848. 15p. 13 plates.

Issued also the same date with 9 additional plates.

182. Diehl, Edith. "National styles of book decoration." (In Bookbinding, its background and technique. N.Y., Rinehart, 1946. p.79-164)

183. Fahey, Herbert and Fahey, Peter. Finishing in hand bookbinding. San Francisco, Priv. printed, 1951. 82p. illus.

184. Husung, Max J. "Graphik und Bucheinband." Maso finiguerra 3:107-21, 289-301. 1938.

185. Josephy, Robert S. "On the use of type ornament in the design of bindings." Publishers' weekly 112:677-81, Sept. 3, 1927.

186. Libri, Guillaume. Monuments inédits ou peu connus...qui se rapportent à l'histoire des arts du dessin considérés dans leur application à l'ornement des livres. London, Dulan, 1862. 14p. 60 plates.

187. Gerlach, Martin, ed. Old book and its decoration from the xv to the xix century: book printing, book illustration and bindings. N.Y., Architectural Book, 1919. 148p. illus.

First published in German in 1915.

188. Marx, Enid. "Pattern papers." Penrose annual 44:51-53. 1950.

189. Michel, Marius. Essai sur la décoration extérieure des livres.
Paris, Morgand et Fatout, 1878. 16p.

190. _____. L'ornementation des reliures modernes. Paris, 1889.
78p. illus. plates.

191. Prideaux, Sarah T. "Some notes on pattern-making." (In Bookbinders and their craft. London, Zaehnsdorf, 1903. p.269-93)

192. Saunier, Charles. Les décorateurs du livre. Paris, Rieder, 1922.
130p. plates.

193. Sekigawa, Sakio. Hon no utsukushisa o motomete. 1979. 211p.
illus.

194. Stephen, George A. Decorative book covers. London, Penrose, 1911.
13p.

     Reprint from Penrose's pictorial annual 1910/11.

195. Uzanne, Octave. La reliure moderne artistique et fantaisiste.
Paris, Rouveyre, 1887. 263p. 72 plates.

196. Zerbe, Walter and Scheuner, Ernst. "Dekorative Bucheinbände im
Wandel der vergangenen fünfundsiebzig Jahre." Schweizerisches Gutenbergmuseum 50:50-53. 1964.

Book Edges

197. Davenport, Cyril J. "The decoration of book-edges." Bibliographica
2:385-407. 1896.

198. Dutter, Vera E. "The ancient art of fore-edge painting." American
artist 33:56-57, Jan. 1969.

199. Nixon, Howard M. "Edges ancient and modern." Times literary
supplement, June 29, 1967, p.588.

     A review of Carl J. Weber's Fore-edge painting (1966).

200. Weber, Carl J. Fore-edge painting; an historical survey of a curious art in book decoration. Irvington-on-Hudson, N.Y., Harvey House,
1966. 223p. illus.

201. _____. A thousand and one fore-edge paintings. Waterville, Me.,
Colby College Press, 1949. 194p. 24 plates.

Doublure

202. Hoedt, Georg. "Geschichte der dublüre von ihren Anfängen bis zur Mitte des 19. Jahrhunderts." Archiv für Buchbinderei 35:26-29, 33-37. 1935.

203. Michelmore, George W. The doublure from its inception in the 16th century to its perfection in the 18th. London, 192? 42p. 6 plates

Embroidery

204. Bodleian Library. Textile and embroidered bindings. Oxford, 1971. 30p. (chiefly illus.) (Bodleian picture books. Special Series no. 2)

205. Davenport, Cyril J. "Embroidered bindings of Bibles in the possession of the British and Foreign Bible Society." Burlington magazine 4:267-80, Mar. 1904.

206. Grolier Club, N.Y. Exhibition of silver, embroidered and curious bookbindings...Apr. 16 to May 9, 1903. N.Y., 1903. 86p.

207. Hughes, Therle. "Books with embroidered bindings." Country life annual, 1966, p.140, 142.

208. Prideaux, Sarah T. "Embroidered book covers." (In An historical sketch of bookbinding. London, 1893. p.140-68)

209. Rothery, Guy C. "Needlework bookbinding." Antiques 19:108-12, Feb. 1931.

210. Rudbeck, Gustaf. Broderade bokband fran aldre tidi svenska samlingar. Stockholm, 1925. 110p. 39 plates.

Endpapers

211. Bierbaum, Otto J. "Künstlerische Vorsatzpapiere." Dekorative Kunst 3:111-29. 1898.

212. Guégan, Bertrand. "History and manufacture of end-papers." Publishers' weekly 116:1755-59, Oct. 5, 1929.

    Translated by Katherine Knight from Arts et métiers graphiques.

213. Hirsch, Olga. "Decorated papers." Penrose annual 51:48-53. 1957.

214. Ingben, Roger. "Decorated papers." Fleuron 2:99-106. 1924.

215. Kersten, Paul. "Das Buntpapiere und seine Verwendung besonders für Bücherfreunde." Zeitschrift für Bücherfreunde 4:169-76, Aug./Sept. 1900.

216. Loring, Rosamond. Decorated book papers. 2d ed. Cambridge, Harvard Univ. Press, 1952. 171p. 16 plates.

217. Mick, Ernst W. Altes Buntpapier. Dortmund, Harenberg, 1979. 175p. 77 colored illustrations.

218. Middleton, Bernard C. "Endpapers." (In A history of English craft bookbinding technique. N.Y., Hafner, 1963. p.33-53)

219. "Value of decorative end papers." Publishers' weekly 118:2124-26, Nov. 1, 1930.

Gilding

220. Barkell, William. En bok om handforgyllning. Stockholm, Bonnier, 1951. 141p. illus.

221. Bodleian Library. Gold-tooled bookbindings. Oxford, 1951. 7p. 24 plates.

222. Brugalla, Emilio. "Gold tooling." (In Smith, Philip. New directions in bookbinding. London, Studio Vista, 1974. p.106-11)

223. Colombini, Guido L. Il doratore rilegatore di libri. Genova-Sampierdarena, Libreria Salesiana, 1949. 441p. illus.

224. Colton, Arthur S. "Gilding book edges." Graphic arts monthly 46:126-28, Oct. 1974.

225. Dewailly. Petit manuel pratique de dorure à l'usage des étudiants. Paris, 1937. 68p.

226. Dudin. L'art du relieur doreur de livres. Paris, Impr. de L. F. Delatour, 1772. 112p. 16 plates.

   Translated into English by R. M. Atkinson and published by Elmete Press in Leeds in 1977.

227. Fache, Jules. La dorure et la décoration des reliures. Paris, 1954. 164p. illus.

228. Fougeroux de Bondaroy, Auguste-Denis. Art de travailler les cuirs dorés et argentés. Paris, 1762. 42p.

229. Gruel, Léon. Conférences sur la reliure et la dorure des livres. Paris, 1903. 69p. illus. facs.

230. Holt, Penelope and Thorpe, Edmond. Gold and books. Privately printed, 1969. 33p. illus.

231. Horn, Otto. Die Technik der Handvergoldung und Lederauflage. 2d ed. Gera, Horn and Patzelt, 1891. 36p. illus. plates.

232. Horne, Herbert P. The binding of books; an essay in the history of gold-tooled bindings. London, Paul, Trench, Trübner, 1894. 224p. plates. 2d ed., rev. and corrected, 1915.

233. Kersten, Paul. Der exakte Bucheinband. Halle, Knapp, 1909. 177p.

234. _____. Das Goldschnittmachen. Halle, Knapp, 1925. 22p. 2d ed., 1936.

235. _____. Lehrbuch der Handvergoldung. Halle, Knapp, 1930. 59p. illus.

236. Kinder, Louis H. Formulas for bookbinders. East Aurora, N.Y., Roycrofters, 1905. 115p. plates.

237. Maul, Johannes and Stockbauer, J. La dorure sur cuir, Reliure, ciselure, et gaufrure en Allemagne. Paris, Rouveyre, 188? 2 vols. 90 plates.

238. Meunier, Charles. Charles Meunier, Paroles d'un practicien pour l'art et la technique du relieur-doreur. Paris, Maison du Livre, 1918. 96p.

239. Nicholson, James B. A manual on the art of bookbinding, containing full instructions in the different branches of forwarding, gilding, and finishing. Phila., Baird, 1856. 318p.

240. Nixon, Howard M. Sixteenth century gold tooled bookbindings in the Pierpont Morgan Library. N.Y., 1971. 263p. illus.

241. Pagnier, Charles and Walter-Jay, Charles. Traité pratique de dorure et de mosaïque sur cuir à l'usage des amateurs. Paris, Publ. de Papyros, 1930. 132p. illus. plates.

242. Peeters, Laurent. Het vergulden op leder voor den boekbinder. Antwerp, Dirix, 1942. 127p.

243. Reber, Adolf. Die Kunst des Vergoldens bei der Buchbinderei. 2d ed. Heilbronn, Landherr, 1845. 16p.

244. Sullivan, Edward. "Design in gold-tooled binding." International studio 24:34-39. 1905.

Jewels

245. Elkind, M. Wieder. "Jewelled bindings 1900-1939." Book collector 24:401-16, autumn 1975.

    About the jewelled leather bindings by Sangorski and Sutcliffe in London.

246. John Rylands Library, Manchester. Catalogue of an exhibition of medieval manuscripts and jewelled book-covers arranged in the main library. With introduction and facsimiles. Manchester, Univ. Press, 1924. 88p. 15 plates.

247. Needham, Paul. "Medieval treasure bindings." (In Twelve centuries
of bookbindings 400-1600. N.Y., Pierpont Morgan Library, Oxford Univ.
Press, 1979. p.24-54)

248. Scott, Temple. "Jeweled bookbindings." International studio
79:19-25, Apr. 1924.

249. Snijder, G. A. "Antique and medieval gems on bookcovers at
Utrecht." Art bulletin 14:5-52, Mar. 1932.

250. Sotheran, firm, booksellers, London. Illustrated catalogue of
magnificent Cosway and jewelled bindings, including an Omar with a
thousand jewels. London, 1911. 10p. 18 plates.

251. Thompson, Lawrence S. "Book and the jewel." Imprimatur 1:10-13,
Jan. 1947.

Marbling

252. Adam, Paul. Das Marmorien des Buchbinders auf Schleimgrund und im
öl- und Kleisterverfahren. 2d ed. Halle, Knapp, 1923. 84p. illus.

253. Boeck, Josef(?) P. Die Marmorierkunst. Vienna, Hartleben, 1880.
80p. illus. 2d ed., 1896.

254. Colton, Arthur S. "Marbling: an ancient art." Graphic arts
monthly 46:124-26, Sept. 1974.

255. Haemmerle, Albert and Hirsch, Olga. Buntpapier. Munich, Callwey,
1961. 250p. 2d ed., 1977. illus. plates.

256. Halfer, Joseph. L'art de la marbrure. Traduction française par
Joseph Grillet et Emile Schultze. Geneva, Grossman, 1894. 126p.

257. _____. Die Fortschritte der Marmorierkunst. 2d ed. Mit Anhang:
Verzierung der Buchschnitte. Stuttgart, W. Leo, 1891. 224p. illus.
plates.

258. _____. The progress of the marbling art. From technical
scientific principles. With a supplement on the decoration of book edges.
Translated by Herman Dieck. 2d ed. Buffalo, Kinder, 1893. 240p. illus.
plates.

259. Hewitt-Bates, James and Halliday, John. Three methods of marbling.
Leicester, Dryad Press, 197? 15p. illus.

260. Kinder, Louis H. Formulas for bookbinders. East Aurora, N.Y.,
Roycrofters, 1905. 115p. plates.

261. Kunckel, Johann. Johannis Kunckelii...ars vitraria experimentalis....
Amsterdam, 1679. 2 parts.

262. Loring, Rosamond. Decorated book papers. 2d ed. Edited by Philip
Hofer. Cambridge, Harvard Univ. Press, 1952. 171p. 16 plates.

263. Nicholson, James B. A manual on the art of bookbinding containing full instructions in the different branches of forwarding, gilding, and finishing. Also the art of marbling book edges and paper. Phila., Baird, 1856. 318p. illus. plates.

264. Schade, J. A. Die Marmorir-Kunst, oder Anweisung den Kamm- und türkischen Marmor anzufertigen, für Buchbinder. Berlin, 1845.

265. Suchanek, Jacob. Das Marmorien der Bücherschnitte. Olmuetz, Suchanek, 1880. 31p.

266. Ulbricht, Gustav. Neuestes Erfahrungen in der Kunst der Schnitt-marmoriens für Buchbinder. Rochlitz, 1855.

267. Weisse, Franz. Die Kunst des Marmoriens. Stuttgart, Hettler, 1940. 11-45, 111p. illus.

Mosaic

268. Grolier Club, N.Y. Mosaic book bindings; a catalogue of an exhibition Jan. 23 to Feb. 22, 1902. N.Y., DeVinne Press, 1902. 53p.

269. Kent, Henry W. "Some notes on mosaic bookbindings." Bibliographer 1:169-80, May 1902.

270. Michon, Louis M. Les reliures mosaïques du xviii^a siècle. Paris, Société de la Reliure Originale, 1956. 125p. plates.

271. Pagnier, Charles and Walter-Jay, Charles. Traité pratique de dorure et de mosaïque sur cuirs à l'usage des amateurs. Paris, Publ. de Papyros, 1930. 132p. illus. plates.

272. Walters, Curtis. "Techniques of mosaic bindings." Bookbinding magazine 22:24-26, Sept. 1935; 22:26-28, Nov. 1935.

6

HISTORY OF BOOKBINDING
FROM ANCIENT TIMES
TO THE PRESENT

Collections of Plates and Illustrations

273. Bachelin-Deflorenne, Antoine. Album de reliures; recueil de cent planches avec notes, par le bibliophile Julien(pseud.) Paris, 1873. 2 vols. 100 plates.

274. Baer, Joseph. Bucheinbände. Bookbindings, historical and decorative. Livres dans de riches reliures. Frankfurt, J. Baer, 1927? 128p. illus. 48 plates.

275. Barthou, Louis. Bibliothèque de Louis Barthou. Paris, Blaizot, 1935-37. 5 vols. illus.

276. Belin, firm, booksellers, Paris. Livres avec riches reliures historiques des xvi⁴,xvii⁴ et xviii⁴ siècles. Paris, 1912. 62 p. plates.

277. Bodleian Library. Fine bindings 1500-1700 from Oxford libraries; catalogue of an exhibition. Oxford, 1968. 144p. 55 illus. 52 plates.

278. Boerner, C. G., firm, Düsseldorf. Kostbare Bucheinbände des xv bis xix Jahrhunderts, beschrieben von Carl Sonntag. Leipzig, 1912. 107p. 52 plates.

279. Bouchot, Henri F. Les reliures d'art a la Bibliothèque Nationale. Paris, Rouveyre, 1888. 51p. 80 plates.

280. Bradac, Ludvik. Uprava vazeb kniznich. 1911. 92p. plates.

281. British Museum. Bookbindings from the library of Jean Grolier; a loan exhibition 23 Sept.-31 Oct. 1965. London, 1965. 75p. plates.

Howard M. Nixon arranged the exhibition and prepared the catalogue.

282. Brunet, Pierre G. La reliure ancienne et moderne. Paris, Daffis, 1878. 2 vols. 116 plates.

283. Brussels. Bibliothèque Royale de Belgique. Exposition de reliures. Brussels, 1930-31. 2 vols.

284. Burlington Fine Arts Club, London. Exhibition of bookbindings; illustrated catalog. London, 1891. 132p. 114 plates.

285. Fletcher, William Y. Foreign bookbindings in the British Museum; illustrations of sixty-three examples selected on account of their beauty or historical interest, with introductions and descriptions by William Younger Fletcher. London, Paul, Trench, Trübner, 1896. 66 leaves. 65 colored plates.

286. Foot, Mirjam M. The Henry Davis gift: a collection of bindings. Vol. 1: Studies in the history of bookbinding. London, British Library, 1978. 352p. plates.

     An important scholarly catalog. See review by Robert Nikirk in Publications of the Bibliographical Society of America 75:498-99, 4th quarter 1981.

287. Grolier Club, N.Y. Catalog of books from the libraries or collections of celebrated bibliophiles and illustrious persons of the past with arms or devices upon the bindings. N.Y., 1895. 75p. illus.

288. Gumachian & Cie. Catalogue de reliures du xve au xixe siècle. Paris, n.d. 180p. 135 plates. (catalog 12)

289. Hoe, Robert. Catalog of the library of Robert Hoe of New York. N.Y., D. Taylor, 1911-12. 8 vols. in 4. plates. facs.

290. _____. One hundred and seventy-six historic and artistic bookbindings 111 from the library of Robert Hoe. N.Y., Dodd, Mead, 1895. 2 vols. plates.

291. Husung, Max J. Bucheinbände aus der Preussischen Staatsbibliothek zu Berlin in historischer folge erläutert. Leipzig, Hiersemann, 1925. 47p. 100 plates.

292. Kersten, Paul. Moderne Entwürfe künstlerische Bucheinbände. Halle, Knapp, 1904-06. 2 vols. 85 colored plates.

293. Kyriss, Ernst. Katalog historischer Einbände des 11 bis 20 Jahrhunderts aus der Württembergischen Landesbibliothek. Stuttgart, 1955. 48p. illus.

294. Kyster, Anker. Bookbindings in the public collections of Denmark. Vol. 1: The Royal Library, Copenhagen. Copenhagen, Levin & Munksgaard, 1938. 128p. 54 plates.

     See review in Library 19:368-74, Dec. 1938.

295. Maggs Bros., London. Bookbindings: historical and decorative. London, 1927. 208p. 116 plates on 66 leaves. (catalog 489)

296. Maxal, Otto. Europäische Einbandkunst aus Mittelalter und Neuzeit. 270 Einbände der Österreichischen National Bibliothek. Graz, Akademische Druck- und Verlagsanstalt, 1970. 94p. 270 plates (some in color).

297. Meunier, Charles. Cent reliures de Bibliothèque Nationale conférence faite...le 18 février 1914. Paris, 1914. 44p. 100 plates.

298. Morgand, Damascene. *Livres dans de riches reliures des 16, 17,18 et 19 siècles.* Paris, 1910. 95p. 50 plates. (sales catalog)

299. Munich. Bayerische Staatsbibliothek. *Bucheinbände aus elf Jahrhunderten, ausgewält und beschrieben von F. Geldner.* Munich, Bruckmann, 1958. 46p. 162 plates. 2d ed., 1959.

300. Needham, Paul. *Twelve centuries of bookbindings 400-1600.* N.Y., Pierpont Morgan Library, Oxford Univ. Press, 1979. 338p. 100 plates.

> Contains 3 indexes: (1) binderies and places of binding,
> (2) provenance: patrons, collectors, owners and (3) bookbindings
> before 1600 in the Pierpont Morgan Library: a preliminary check-
> list.

301. Nixon, Howard M. *Broxbourne Library. Styles and designs of bookbindings from the twelfth to the twentieth century.* London, Maggs Bros., 1956. 250p. facs.

> Appendix B contains a long list of binders for signed bindings in
> the Broxbourne Library, p.242-44.

302. Pearson, J. and Co. *Very choice books, including an extremely important series of historical bindings....* London, 1901? 146p. 74 plates.

303. Pickering and Chatto, firm, London. *Illustrated catalog of old and rare books, illuminated manuscripts, specimens of fine old and modern bindings....* London, 1906-08? 712p. plates.

304. Quaritch, Bernard. *Catalog of English and foreign bookbindings offered for sale.* London, 1921. 76p. 79 plates.

305. _____. *A collection of facsimiles from examples of historic or artistic bookbinding.* London, 1889. 36p. 103 plates.

306. Rahir, Edouard. *La bibliothèque de feu Edouard Rahir, ancien libraire.* Paris, Lefrançois, 1930-38. 6 vols. plates.

307. _____. *La collection Dutuit. Livres et manuscrits.* Paris, Morgand, 1899. 328p. facs. plates.

308. Schmidt, Adolf. *Bucheinbände aus dem xiv-xix Jahrhundert in der Landesbibliothek zu Darmstadt ausgewählt und beschrieben von Dr. Adolf Schmidt.* Leipzig, Hiersemann, 1921. 41p. 100 plates.

309. Techener, Jacques-Joseph and Techener, Léon. *Histoire de la bibliophile. Reliures. Recherches sur les bibliothèques des plus célèbres amateurs. Armorial des bibliophiles.* Paris, J. Techener, 1861-64. 10 parts. plates.

310. Vienna. Nationalbibliothek. *Bucheinbände; auswahl von technisch und geschichtich Bemerkenwertenstücken. Einleitung von Theodor Gottlieb.* Vienna, Schroll, 1910. 100 illus.

311. Weale, William H. Bookbindings and rubbings of bindings in the
National Art Library, S. Kensington Muscum. London, Printed for HMSO
by Eyre and Spottiswoode, 1894-98. 2 vols. in 1.

312. Westendorp, Karl. Die Kunst der alten Buchbinder. Halle, 1909.
26p. 132 plates.

313. Wheatley, Henry B. Remarkable bindings in the British Museum.
Described by Henry B. Wheatley. London, Gruel and Engelmann, 1889.
143p. 62 plates.

314. Zimmermann, Carl. Bucheinbände aus dem Bücherschätze der K. Bibliothek zu Dresden. Leipzig, 1887. 2 vols. 101 photographs.

General Works

315. Andrews, William L. A short historical sketch of the art of bookbinding...with a description of the prominent styles. N.Y., 1895. 45p.
illus.

316. Brassington, William S. A history of the art of bookbinding, with
some account of the books of the ancients. London, Stock, 1894. 277p.
illus.

317. Cockerell, Douglas. "The development of bookbinding methods.
Coptic influence." Library 13:1-19. 1932.

318. Colombini, Guido L. Gli artefici del libro, antico e moderno.
Florence, Scuola Tipografica, 1935. 361p. illus. plates.

319. Colombo, Pio. La legatura artistica. Storia e critica. Rome,
1952. 177p. plates.

320. Culot, Paul. "Bookbinding from the sixteenth century to the
present." (In Vervliet, Hendrik D. L., ed. The book through five thousand years. London, Phaidon, 1972. p.458-85)

321. Cundall, Joseph, ed. On bookbindings ancient and modern. London,
Bell, 1881. 132p. 22 plates.

322. Diehl, Edith. Bookbinding, its background and technique. N.Y.,
Rinehart, 1946. 2 vols. illus. plates.

323. Dutton, Meirick. Historical sketch of bookbinding as an art.
Norwood, Holliston Mills, 1926. 144p.

324. "Encuadernacion." Enciclopedia universal ilustrada 19:1197-1235.

325. Fischer, Ernst F. Bokhandets historia. Stockholm, 1922. 80p.
plates.

326. Gerlach, Martin, ed. Das alte Buch und siene Ausstattung vom 15
bis zum 19 Jahrhundert. Buchdruck, Buchschmuck, und Einbände. Vienna,
1915. 148p. illus.

327. Hamanová, Pavlína. Z dějin knizni vazby od nejstarších dob do konce xix. stol. Prague, 1959. 275p. plates.

328. Harrison, Thomas. The bookbinding craft and industry; an outline of its history, development and technique. London, Pitman, 1926. 128p. 2d ed., 1930.

329. Harthan, John P. Bookbindings. 2d ed. London, HMSO, 1961. 33p. 79 plates. (Victoria and Albert Museum. Illustrated booklet no. 2)

330. Helwig, Hellmuth. Handbuch der Einbandkunde. Hamburg, Maximilian-Gesellschaft, 1953-55. 3 vols.

   Vol. 1 has essays on history, conservation, and cataloging of bindings. Bibliographies follow the essays. Einführing in die Einbandkunde (Stuttgart, 1970) is the title of the revision of vol. 1. The other two volumes are biographical reference works. (see REFERENCE WORKS)

331. Hoe, Robert. A lecture on bookbinding as a fine art, delivered before the Grolier Club, Feb. 26, 1885. N.Y., Grolier Club, 1886. 36p. illus.

332. Hofer, Philip. "Binding styles; a foreword to an exhibition in the Spencer room." Bulletin of the New York Public Library 38:607-19, Aug. 1934.

333. Loubier, Hans. Der Bucheinband in alter und neuer Zeit. Berlin, Seamann, 1903. 186p. illus.

334. _____. Der Bucheinband von seinen Anfängen bis zum Ende des 18. Jahrhunderts. 2d ed. Leipzig, Klinkhardt & Biermann, 1926. 272p. illus.

335. McCarthy, William H. "An outline of the history of bookbinding." Dolphin no. 3:447-68, 1938.

336. Marinis, Tammaro de et al. "Legatura." Enciclopedia italiana 20:742-52, 1933.

337. Matthews, Brander. Bookbindings old and new; notes of a book-lover, with an account of the Grolier Club of New York. N.Y., Macmillan, 1895. 342p. illus.

338. Nilsson, Axel R. Bokbandsdekorens Stilutveckling. Goteborg, 1922. 161p.

339. Nixon, Howard. The development of certain styles of bookbinding. London, Private Libraries Association, 1963. 16p. illus.

340. Peeters, Laurent. Handbook voor den boekbinder. Antwerp, Standard-Boekhandel, 1946. 252p. illus. plates.

341. Pešina, Jaroslav. Knizni vazba v minulosti. Prague, 1939. 44p. 50 plates.

342. Prideaux, Sarah T. Bookbinders and their craft. London,
Zaehnsdorf, 1903. 298p. illus.

343. _____. An historical sketch of bookbinding, with a chapter on
early stamped bindings by E. Gordon Duff. London, 1893. 303p.

>"The chief part of the book was written as an introduction to the
>cataloque of the exhibition of bindings held at the Burlington
>Fine Arts Club in the summer of 1891."--Preface. Contains a
>bibliography on binding, p.251-94.

344. Shoji, Sensui. Shoseki sotei no rekishi to jissa. 1929. 399p.

345. Thévenin, Léon and Lemierre, Georges. Les arts du livre. IV.
Histoire de la reliure. Paris, Société des Amis du Livre Moderne, 1915.
107p. plates.

346. Thomas, Alan G. "Bookbinding." (In Great books and book collectors. N. Y., Putnam, 1975. p.64-89)

347. Walters Art Gallery, Baltimore. The history of bookbinding 525-
1950; an exhibition held at the Baltimore Museum of Art, Nov. 12, 1957
to Jan. 12, 1958. Organized by the Walters Art Gallery. Baltimore,
1957. 275p. 106 plates.

348. Zahn, Otto. On art binding. Memphis, Toof, 1904. 54p. 12 plates.

Early Years to the Twelfth Century

349. Braunfels, Wolfgang. Die Welt der Karolinger und ihre Kunst.
Munich, Callwey, 1968. 402p. illus.

>Contains illustrations of book covers and bindings. Bibliography
>at end of volume (p.392-95) has many useful titles.

350. Christ, Karl. "Karolingische Bibliothekseinbände." (In
Festschrift Georg Leyh. Leipzig, Harrassowitz, 1937. p.82-104)

351. Davenport, Cyril J. "Manuscripts and their bindings." (In
Beautiful books. London, Methuen, 1929. p.1-33)

352. Hobson, Geoffrey D. "Further notes on Romanesque bindings."
Library 15:161-211. 1934.

353. Regemorter, Berthe van. "Le codex relié depuis son origine jusqu'au
haut moyen-âge." Le moyen âge 61:1-26. 1955.

354. _____. "La reliure byzantine." Revue d'archéologie et
d'histoire de l'art 36:99-162. 1967.

355. _____. "La reliure des manuscrits grecs et de l'Egypte."
Scriptorium 8:3-23. 1954.

356. Ribstein, Ann. "Decorated Carolingian book covers; an icono-
graphical study." M. A. thesis, Univ. of Chicago, 1975. 132p.

357. Steenbock, Frauke. Der kirchliche Prachteinband in frühen Mittelalter von Anfängen bis zum Beginn der Gothik. Berlin, Deutsche Verlag
für Kunstwissenschaft, 1965. 237p. 176 plates.

358. Theophilus. The various arts. Translated from the Latin with
introduction and notes by C. R. Dodwell. London, Nelson, 1961. 171, 171,
175-78p.

    An account of the experience of a monastic artist, probably of the
    12th century, in north-west Germany. The work is a treatise on
    medieval skills and crafts, including the working of silver and
    gold, the making of enamel, gilding, and painting in books. Mr.
    Dodwell provides an excellent introduction to his translation of
    De Diuersis, the original title.

Gothic

359. Bollert, Martin. Lederschnittbände des xiv Jahrhunderts. Leipzig,
Hiersemann, 1925. 77p. facs.

360. Cennini, Cennino. Il libro dell'arte. New Haven, Yale Univ.
Press, 1932-33. 2 vols. illus. facs.

    A fifteenth century work (1437) edited and translated by Daniel
    V. Thompson. It is "the most informative source on the methods,
    techniques and attitudes of medieval artists." Encyclopedia
    Britannica, 15th ed. (1981), Micropedia 2:677.

361. Cockerell, Sydney. "The binding of manuscripts." (In Lamb, Cecil M.
The calligrapher' handbook. London, Faber and Faber, 1956. p.199-223)

362. Egbert, Virginia W. The medieval artist at work. Princeton,
Princeton Univ. Press, 1967. 94p. illus. plates.

    Contains illustrations showing artists at work in the middle ages:
    illuminator, panel painter, ivory carver, goldsmith, and sculptor.

363. Ellard, Gerald. "Some notes on medieval mass books."
Ecclesiastical review 85:344-62, Oct. 1931.

364. Goldschmidt, Ernst P. Gothic and Renaissance book bindings.
Exemplified and illustrated from the author's collection. London, Benn,
1928. 2 vols.

365. Kyriss, Ernst. Der verzierte europäische Einband vor der Renaissance. Stuttgart, Hettler, 1957. 40p. 16 plates.

    An excerpt from Verzierte gotische Einbände in alten deutsche
    Sprachgebiet (4 vols., 1951-58)

366. Lacroix, Paul. "Reliure." (In Les arts au moyen-âge at à l'époque de la renaissance. 5th ed. Paris, Firmin, Didot, 1874. p.489-504)

367. Loubier, Hans. "Der kirchliche Prachtband des frühen Mittelatlers (bis zum 13. Jahrhundert)" (In Der Bucheinband. 2d ed. Leipzig, Klinkhardt and Biermann, 1926. p.23-54)

368. _____. "Der Prachtband des späten Mittelalters (14 und 15. Jahrhundert)." (In Der Bucheinband. 2d ed. Leipzig, Klinkhardt and Biermann, 1926. p.55-65)

369. Lowe, Elias A., ed. Codices Latini antiquiores. Oxford, Clarendon Press, 1934-66. 11 vols. facs.

370. Mazal, Otto. Buchkunst der Gotik. Graz, Akademische Druck- und Verlagsanstalt, 1975. 253p. 54 leaves of plates.

371. _____. "Medieval bookbinding." (In Vervliet, Hendrik D. L., ed. The book through five thousand years. London, Phaidon, 1972. p.314-40)

372. Petersen, Dag-Ernst. Millelalterliche Bucheinbände der Herzog August Bibliothek. Wolfenbuttel, 1975. 91p. illus.

373. Deleted

374. Steenbock, Frauke. Der kirchliche Prachteinband in frühen Mittel- alter von den Anfängen bis zum Beginn der Gotik. Berlin, Deutsche Verlag für Kunstwissenschaft, 1965. 237p. 176 plates.

375. Vezin, Jean. Evolution des techniques de la reliure médiévale. Paris, Bibliothèque Nationale, 1973. 17p. illus.

Renaissance

376. Adam, Paul. "Der Einfluss der Klosterarbeit auf die Einbandkunst." (In Buch und Bucheinband. Aufsätze und graphische Blätter zum 60. Geburtstage von Hans Loubier. Leipzig, Hiersemann, 1923. p.148-69)

377. Belin, firm, booksellers, Paris. Livres des xve and xvie siècles dans leurs reliures originales. Paris, 1914. 142p. 92 plates.

378. Butsch, Albert F. Die Bücherornamentik der Hoch- und Spätrenais- sance. Leipzig, Hirth, 1881. 56p. 118 plates.

379. _____. Die Bücherornamentik der Renaissance. Leipzig, Hirth, 1878. 72p. 108 plates.

380. Fischer, Wolfgang G. Die Blütezeit der Einbandkunst; Studien über den Stil des 15. bis 18. Jahrhunderts. Leipzig, Stein, 1935. 73p.

381. Gasiorowska, Maria J. "Ikonografia swiecka na oprawach 16 i 17 w." Rocznik biblioteki narodowej 6:315-37. 1970.

     A world iconography of bookbinding of the 16th and 17th centuries.

382. Goldschmidt, Ernst P. Gothic and Renaissance bookbindings.
Exemplified and illustrated from the author's collection. London, Benn,
1928. 2 vols.

383. _____. "The study of early bookbinding." (In Bibliographical
Society, London. The Bibliographical Society. Studies in retrospect,
1892-1942. London, 1945. p.175-84)

384. Grolier Club, N.Y. A catalog of an exhibition of renaissance bookbindings held at the Grolier Club from Dec. 17, 1936 to Jan. 17, 1937.
N.Y., 1937. 68p. 16 plates.

385. Knaus, Hermann. "Einbandstempel des 14. Jahrhunderts." (In
Festschrift Ernst Kyriss. Stuttgart, Hettler, 1961. p.55-71)

386. Kristeller, Paul. "Woodcuts as bindings." Bibliographica
1:249-51. 1895.

387. Pierpont Morgan Library, N.Y. Sixteenth century gold-tooled bookbindings in the Pierpont Morgan Library. By Howard M. Nixon. N.Y.,
1971. 263p. illus.

388. Prideaux, Sarah T. "Early stamped bindings." (In Bookbinders
and their craft. London, Zaehnsdorf, 1903. p.163-210)

389. Schunke, Ilse. "Farbige Bandwerkeinbände in der Renaissance."
Gutenberg Jahrbuch 1971, p.360-72.

390. _____. "Von Menschen und Einbänden in der Renaissance."
Librarium 2:2-23. 1968.

391. _____, ed. Beiträge zum Rollen- und Platteneinband im 16.
Jahrhundert. Leipzig, Harrassowitz, 1937. 408p. 14 plates.

392. Wallis, Alfred. Examples of the bookbinder's art of the xvi and
xvii centuries; selected chiefly from the royal continental libraries.
With descriptions and an introduction by A. Wallis. Exeter [London]
J. G. Commin, 1890. 13p. 40 plates.

393. Weale, William H. and Taylor, Lawrence. Early stamped bookbindings
in the British Museum. London, British Museum, 1922. 171p. 32 plates.

Seventeenth and Eighteenth Centuries

394. Barber, Giles. "Continental paper wrappers and publishers' bindings in the 18th century." Book collector 24:37-48. 1975.

395. Fischer, Wolfgang G. Die Blütezeit der Einbandkunst; Studien über
den Stil des 15. bis 18. Jahrhunderts. Leipzig, Stein, 1935. 73p.

396. Michon, Louis M. Les reliures mosaïquées du xviiie siècle. Paris,
Société de la Reliure Originale, 1956. 124p. 45 plates.

397. Rhein, Adolf. "Die frühen Verlagseinbände; eine technische
Entwicklung 1735-1850." Gutenberg Jahrbuch 1962, p.519-32.

Nineteenth Century

398. Adams, Charles M. "Illustrated publishers' bindings." Bulletin of the New York Public Library 41;607-11, Aug. 1937.

399. Béraldi, Henri. La reliure du xix siècle. Paris, Conquet, 1895-97. 4 vols. 283 colored plates.

400. Callen, Anthea. "Hand-printing, bookbinding and illustration." (In Women artists of the arts and crafts movement 1870-1914. N.Y., Pantheon Books, 1979. p.180-211)

401. Chytil, Karel and Borovsky, F. A. Bucheinbände von 18 Jahrhundert bis in der neueste Zeit. Prague, 1904. 30 plates.

402. Comparato, Frank E. Books for the millions; a history of the men whose methods and machines packaged the printed word. Harrisburg, Pa., Stackpole Co., 1971. 374p. illus.

403. Gaskell, Philip. "Edition binding." (In A new introduction to bibliography. Oxford, Clarendon Press, 1972. p.231-50)

404. Harvard University. Houghton Library. Dept. of Printing and Graphic Arts. The turn of a century 1885-1910. Art nouveau--Jugendstil books. Cambridge, 1970. 124p. illus.

405. Kersten, Paul. Moderne Stempel und Bucheinbände. Magdeburg, Dornemann, 1906. 71p. illus. plates.

406. Leighton, Douglas. Modern bookbinding; a survey and a prospect. N.Y., Oxford Univ. Press, 1935. 63p.

407. Matthews, Brander. "Bookbindings of the present: notes of a book-lover." Century magazine 48:277-90, June 1894.

        Includes illustrations of bindings by Zaehnsdorf, Cobden-Sanderson, William Matthews, Ruban, and Petit.

408. Matthews, William. Modern bookbinding practically considered. A lecture read before the Grolier Club of New York, Mar. 25, 1885, with additions and new illustrations. N.Y., Grolier Club, 1889. 96p. illus. facs.

409. Michel, Marius. L'ornementation des reliures modernes. Paris, 1889. 78p. illus.

410. Modern book-bindings and their designers. N.Y., John Lane, 1900. 82p. illus. colored plates.

411. Prideaux, Sarah T. Modern bookbindings, their design and decoration. London, Constable, 1906. 131p. illus.

412. Sadleir, Michael. The evolution of publishers' binding styles 1770-1900. London, Constable, 1930. 95p.

413. Société des Bibliophiles et Iconophiles de Belgique. La reliure romantique. Exposition à la Bibliothèque Albert 1ᵉʳ, du 12 octobre au 19 novembre 1961. Brussels, 1961. 87p. 32 plates.

414. Thoma, A. Moderne Entwürfe für Buchdecken. Leipzig, Hedeler, 1902. 94 plates.

415. Uzanne, Octave. La reliure moderne artistique et fantaisiste. Paris, Rouveyre, 1887. 263p. 72 plates.

Twentieth Century

416. Briggs, Victor H. and Briggs, Ernest L. Twentieth century cover designs. Chicago, Inland Printer, 1902. 59p., 46p., 37 leaves. illus.

     Contains essays by F. M. Sheldon, W. G. Bowdoin, J. S. Hodge,
     R. R. Adams and others.

417. Brugalla, Emilio. "Bookbinders search for new design." Craft horizons 14:28-31, Sept. 1954.

418. Clough, Eric A. "Perfect binding; a new development." Library Association record 51:310-12, Oct. 1949.

419. Cohen, Philip. "Bookbinding today." Times literary supplement 72:1518-19, Dec. 7, 1973.

420. Colton, Arthur S. "Modern book cover decoration." Graphic arts monthly 44:108-12, Apr. 1972.

421. _____. "Today's binding lines." Graphic arts monthly 47:86-87, Feb. 1975.

422. Cosden, Thomas B. "Trends in bindery automation." (In Graphic arts manual. N.Y., Arno Press, Musarts Publishing Corp., 1980. p.571-74)

423. Cretté, Georges. "Distinctive designs in hand-tooled bookbindings." Creative art 7:378-81, Nov. 1930.

424. Dawson, Charles E. "Modern book covers from the designer's point of view." Penrose pictorial annual 14:177-84. 1908/09.

425. Flower, Desmond. "A survey of modern binding." Signature 9:19-35, July 1938.

426. Hand bookbinding today; an international art; an exhibition organized by the San Francisco Museum of Modern Art in cooperation with the Hand Bookbinders of California. San Francisco, San Francisco Museum of Art, 1978. 91p. illus.

427. Harrison, Thomas. "Contemporary bindings: a commentary." Penrose annual 44:71-74. 1949.

428. Harvard University. Houghton Library. Dept. of Printing and
Graphic Arts. The turn of a century 1885-1910. Art nouveau--Jugendstil
books. Cambridge, 1970. 124p. illus.

429. Hunt Institute for Botanical Documentation. The tradition of fine
binding in the twentieth century; a catalogue of an exhibition 12 Nov.
1979 to 15 Feb. 1980. Pittsburgh, the Hunt Institute and Davis and
Warde, 1979. 129p. plates.

430. Istel, Paul. "Reliures de notre temps depuis plus de 4 siècles."
Arts et métiers graphiques, special no. 26:67-75, Nov. 15, 1931.

431. Johnston, Paul. "Fine books and the process of book binding."
(In Biblia-Typographica. N.Y., Covici, Friede, 1930. p. 286-92)

432. La Vesser, Gilbert. "Progress in small bindery operations,
mechanical binding and finishing." (In Printing progress, a mid-century
report. N.Y., International Association of Printing House Craftsmen,
1959. p.341-46)

433. McMurtrie, Douglas C. Design in bookbinding, as represented in
exhibits at the sixth triennial exhibition of graphic arts at Milan,
Italy in 1936. Chicago, Priv. printed, 1938. 24p. illus.

434. Mansfield, Edgar. "New directions in bookbinding." Graphis
15:350-57, July 1959.

435. Marx, Enid. "Pattern papers." Penrose annual 44:51-53. 1950.

436. Mason, John. "The future of fine bindings." Printing review
16:12-15, spring 1952.

437. Massman, Robert E. "Binding miniature books is no small job."
Library scene 9:2-5, Mar. 1980.

438. Newdigate, Bernard H. The art of the book. London, Studio, 1938.
104p. illus.

439. The print casebooks; the best in covers. Wash., D.C., R. C. Publications, 1975-

440. Rauch, Nicolas. "Reliures." (In Les peintres et le livre. Geneva,
Rauch, 1957. p.219-32)

441. Rebsamen, Werner. "Binding technology." Publishers' weekly
214:30, 32, Dec. 4, 1978.

442. _____. "A study of simple binding methods." Library scene
9:20-25, Mar. 1980.

443. Smith, Philip. New directions in bookbinding. Cincinnati, Van
Nostrand Reinhold, 1975. 208p. illus.

7

HISTORY OF BOOKBINDING
IN THE
COUNTRIES OF THE WORLD

Austria

444. Alker, Hugo. "Beutelbücher in Österreich." Gutenberg Jahrbuch 1955, p.229-35.

445. Eichler, Ferdinand. "Lederschnittbände in Österreich." (In Leyh, Georg, ed. Aufsaetze Fritz Milkau gewidmet. Leipzig, Hiersemann, 1921. p.86-94)

446. Eisler, Max. Dagobert Peche. Vienna, Gerlach and Wiedling, 1925. 43p. 110 plates.

447. Holme, Charles, ed. The art-revival in Austria. Studio, special no., 1906. [56p.] illus.

    Contains 3 illustrations of bindings by the Wiener Werkstätte and one by Josef Hoffmann.

448. Holter, Kurt. "Beiträge zur Geschichte des Lederschnitt-Einbändes in Niederösterreich." Gutenberg Jahrbuch 39:334-42. 1964.

449. _____. "Der Lederschnitteinband in Oberösterreich." (In Festschrift Ernst Kyriss. Stuttgart, Hettler, 1961. p.83-121)

450. _____. "Romanische Bucheinband des 12.Jahrhunderts aus Kloster Lambach, Oberösterreich." Gutenberg Jahrbuch 1965, p.343-47)

451. _____. "Zum gotischen Bucheinband in Österreich. Bemalte Einbände aus Kloster Garten." Gutenberg Jahrbuch 1956, p.288-98.

452. Levetus, A. S. "The art of the book in Austria." (In Holme, Charles, ed. The art of the book. London, Studio, 1914. p.203-30)

453. _____. "Contemporary Austrian bookbindings." Studio 88:255-56, Nov. 1924.

454. Mazal, Otto. "Bucheinbände." (In Ausstellung: Gotik in Österreich von der Stadt Krems an der Donau, 19.mai bis 15.octobre 1967, Minoriten Kirche Krems-Stein Niederösterreich. 3d ed. Krems an der Donau, 1967. p.262-74)

    Plates 62-65 contain illustrations of bindings. A good bibliography follows the article.

455. Menzel, Maris. Wiener Buchbinder der Barockzeit. Graz, 1972.
130p. 16 plates.

456. Rozsondai, Marianne. "Wiener Dominikanereinbände in der Bibliothek
der Ungarischen Akademie der Wissenschaften." Gutenberg Jahrbuch 1981,
p.234-44.

457. Tinhof, M. "Die Wiener Buchbinder von 1600 bis 1750." Dissertation,
Univ. of Vienna, 1967. 161p.

458. Vienna. Österreichisches Museum für Angewandte Kunst. Die Wiener
Werkstätte modernes Kunsthandwerk von 1903-1932. Vienna, 1967. 100p.
80p. of illus. (exhibit catalog)

Belgium

459. Brassinne, Joseph. La reliure mosane. Liège, Cormaux, 1912. 44p.
78 plates.

460. Colin, Georges. "Reliures belges du xix^{e}siècle." Le livre et
l'estampe 1958, p.50-60.

461. Dhanens, E. "Le scriptorum des Hieronymites à Gand." Scriptorium
23:361-79. 1969.

     The bindings were made by the Hieronymites in Ghent, 1429-1569.
     The religious order is also known as the hermits of St. Jerome.

462. Dubois d'Enghien, Hector. La reliure en Belgique au 19^{e}siècle.
Bruxelles, Leclercq, 1954. 251p. plates.

463. Godenne, Willy. La reliure ancienne en Belgique. Brussels, 1962.
25p.

464. Hammacher, A. M. "Van de Velde et le livre." (In Le monde de
Henry van de Velde. Paris, Librairie Hachette, 1967. p.90-99)

     The book contains a long bibliography, p.342-44.

465. Khnopff, Fernand. "Belgian bookbinding." Studio, special winter
no. 1899-1900, p. 68-73.

466. Jonghe D'Ardoye, Theodore A. de. Armorial belge du bibliophile.
Brussels, 1930. 3 vols.

467. "Painting and the graphic arts." (In Art nouveau, Belgium, France.
Catalog of an exhibition organized by the Institute for the Arts, Rice
University and the Art Institute of Chicago. By Yvonne Brunhammer et al.
Houston, Institute for the Arts, Rice Univ., 1976. p.40-93)

     Contains several cover illustrations by Henry van de Velde, the
     famous Belgian architect, designer, and painter.

468. Pierron, S. "La reliure en Belgique au moyen âge." La chronique
graphique 10:2721-25. 1935.

469. Schunke, Ilse. Die Einbände der Palatina in der Vaticanischen
Bibliothek. Vatican City, Bibliotheca Apostolica Vaticana, 1962. 2 vols.
illus.

    Contains bindings from workshops in Louvain and Antwerp.

470. Verheyden, Prosper. "De paneelstempel van Wouter van Duffel,
priester, boekbinder te Antwerpen." Gulden passer 15:1-36. 1937.

471. _____. "La reliure en Brabant." (In Le livre, l'estampe,
l'édition en Brabant du xv^a au xix^a siècle. Gembloux, Belgium, Ducolot,
1935. p.141-88)

472. Li, Yao-nan. "Chung-kuo shu chuang k'ao (the evolution of bookbinding in China)." T'u shu kuan hsüeh chi k'an 4:207-16, June 1930.

473. Martinique, Edward G. "Binding and preservation of Chinese double-
leaved books." Library quarterly 43:227-36, July 1973.

474. _____. "Chinese traditional bookbinding; a study of its evolution and techniques." Master's thesis, Univ. of Chicago, 1972.

Czechoslovakia

475. Kneide, Pravoslav. "Tscheshische buchkultur nach 1945."
Marginalien no. 60, p.46-57.

476. Nuska, Bohumil. "Die Beziehungen des böhmischen Renaissancebuchein-
bändes zu den Nachbarländer." Zeitschriften für Bibliothekswesen 75:481-
94. 1961.

477. _____. "Evidence materialu pro soupis českých renesančních
vazeb." Historická knižni vazba 1:80-90. 1962.

478. _____. "Počáty české renesanční knizní vazby." Umění 10:469-93.
1962.

    The beginning of Bohemian renaissance bindings.

479. _____. "Typologie českých renesančnich vazeb. Terminologie,
slohové určováni a datováni materiálu." Historická knžní vazba 1964/65,
p.19-145; 1966, p.184-89.

Denmark

Early years to 1900

480. Björjeson, Ingeborg. Indbinding av boger; dansk og fransk technik.
Copenhagen, 1936. 151p.

481. Bröchner, Georg. "Danish bookbinding." Studio, special winter no. 1899-1900, p.74-78.

482. Danish eighteenth century bindings 1730-1780. With an introduction by Sofus Larsen and Anker Kyster. Copenhagen, Levin and Munksgaard, 1930. 52p. 102 plates.

483. Madsen, Karl J. Thorvald Bindesbøll. Copenhagen, 1943. 201p. illus.

   Contains a long bibliography, p.171-201.

484. Meier-Graefe, A. J. "Some recent continental bookbindings." Studio 9:37-50, Oct. 1895.

   Contains 4 facsimiles of bindings by Hans Tégner, 19th century Danish painter, illustrator, and designer of bindings.

485. Nielsen, Carl P. and Berg, Rasmus. Danmarks bogbinders gennen 400 aar. Copenhagen, 1926. 273p. illus.

20th Century

486. Janner, Ostwald. Bogbinder August Sandgren 1893-1934. Copenhagen, Sandgren-Klubben, 1949. 37p. illus.

487. Michelsen, P. U. and Wolf, E. C. "Anker Kyster." Nyt tidsskrift for kunstindustri 12:85-90, June 1939.

488. Park, Henrik. Modern Danish bindings. Copenhagen, Anker Kysters, 1950. 31p. illus.

489. _____. Moderne danske bindtyper. Copenhagen, Fischer, 1949. 53p. illus.

490. _____ and Thomsen, Carl. Bogbinderen August Sandgren. Copenhagen, 1952. 114p.

491. Petersen, Johannes. Jakob Baden 1861-1940. Nyt tidsskrift for kunstindustri, vol. 30, 1940. 129p.

492. "Renaissance in Danish bookbinding." Bookbinding and book production 55:42-43, Feb. 1952.

493. Roos, C. "August Sandgren 1893-1934." Bogvennen 1935, p.61-66.

494. Trier Morch, Ibi. L'art de la reliure au Danemark. Exposition à la Maison du Danemark, du 6 novembre au 2 décembre. Paris, 1968? 46p. illus.

495. Wolf, E. C. "Danske bogbind fra de sidste 75 ar." Bogvennen 1962/63, p.32-48.

496. _____. "Danish bookbinding of today." Danish Foreign Office journal no. 213:134-38, Oct. 1938.

497. Zahle, Erik. "Dansk bogbinderei i vor tid." Bogvennen 2:54-94.
1927.

Egypt

498. Adam, Paul. "Der koptische Einband in Berlin." Archiv für Buchbinderei 11:177-81, Mar. 1912.

499. Atil, Esin. "Illuminated manuscripts." (In Renaissance of Islam;
art of the Mamlucks. Washington, D.C., Smithsonian Institution Press,
1981. p.24-49)

500. Bell, Harold I. "Early codices from Egypt." Library 10:303-13,
July 1909.

501. Cramer, Maria. "Einbände und Kassetten." (In Koptische Buchmalerei.
Recklinghausen, Bongers, 1964. p.125-34)

502. Eisen, Gustavus A. "The art of book covers." International studio
80:91-98, Nov. 1924.

     Contains illustrations for 3 Egyptian book covers.

503. Grohmann, Adolf. [Coptic bindings] (In Arnold, Thomas and Grohmann,
Adolf. The Islamic book. Paris, Pegasus Press, 1929. p.34-44)

504. Haldane, Duncan. Mamluk painting. Warminster, England, Aris and
Phillips, 1978. 107p. 72 illus.

     Contains a very brief description of binding for each manuscript.

505. Hobson, Geoffrey D. "Some early bindings and binders' tools."
Library 19:202-49, Sept. 1938.

     Part of the article (p.202-14) is on Coptic bindings.

506. Ibscher, Hugo. "Alte koptische Einbände." Archiv für Buchbinderei
11:113-16. 1911.

507. _____. "Coptic bookbinding in Egypt." Berliner museen 49:86-90.
1928.

508. Lamacraft, C. T. "Early bookbindings from a Coptic monastery."
Library 20:214-33, Sept. 1939.

509. Regemorter, Berthe van. "La reliure des manuscrits grecs et de
l'Egypte." Scriptorium 8, no.1:3-23. 1954.

510. _____. Some early bindings from Egypt in the Chester Beatty
Library. Dublin, Hodges, Figgis, 1958. 26p. 13 plates.

Finland

511. Meier-Graefe, A. J. "Some recent continental bookbindings."
Studio 9:37-50, Oct. 1895.

512. Puokka, Jaakko. "Über finnisches Buchbinden vom Ende des 17.
Jahrhundert bis zum Anfäng des 19. Jahrhundert." Gutenberg Jahrbuch
37:512-18. 1962.

France

Reference Works

513. Carteret, Léopold. Le trésor du bibliophile: livres illustrés
modernes 1875 à 1945. Paris, Librairie L. Carteret, 1946-48. 5 vols.
facs.

   Vol. 2 has a chapter on binding and binders of the 19th and 20th
   centuries, p.1-26.

514. _____. Le trésor du bibliophile romantique et moderne 1801-1875.
Paris, L. Carteret, 1924-28. 4 vols. illus. facs. 5th vol., 1946-48.

   Contains facsimiles of a great many paper covers.

515. Davies, Hugh W., ed. Catalogue of early French books in the
library of C. Fairfax Murray. London, Holland Press, 1961. 2 vols. illus.

   Reprint of 1910 ed. The period is 1475-1692. Gives brief descriptions for bindings. Contains a great many illustrations.

516. Devauchelle, Roger. La reliure en France de ses origines à nos
jours. Paris, Rousseau-Girard, 1959-61. 3 vols. plates.

   In each volume the text is followed by a long bibliography, a list
   of French binders, and many plates.

517. Fourny, Roger. "Petit lexique de termes professionels." (In
Manuel de reliure. 2d ed. Paris, Librairie Polytechnique Béranger,
Dep. Technique des Presses de la Cité, 1965. p.270-83)

518. Gruel, Léon. Manuel historique et bibliographique de l'amateur de
reliures. Paris, Gruel and Engelmann, 1887-1905. 2 vols. illus.
plates. facs.

519. Kolb, Albert. Bibliographie des französischen Buches im 16.
Jahrhundert. Wiesbaden, Harrassowitz, 1966-71. 2 vols.

   Bibliography on binding in vol. 1, p.227-45, and vol. 2, p.80-84.

520. Lonchamp, Frédéric C. Manuel du bibliophile français (1470-1920).
Paris, Librairie des Bibliophiles, 1927. 2 vols.

521. Olivier, Eugène et al. Manuel de l'amateur de reliures armoriées françaises. Paris, Bosse,1924-38. 30 vols. illus.

522. Ramsden, Charles. French bookbinders 1789-1848. London, Humphries, 1950. 228p. plates.

   Contains a separate list of binders working outside of Paris, p.13-17.

523. Roquet, Antoine E. Les relieurs français (1500-1800). Biographie critique et anecdotique, précédé de l'histoire de la communauté des relieurs et doreurs de la ville de Paris et sur les styles de reliure. Par Ernest Thoinan [pseud.] Paris, Paul, Huard and Guillemin, 1893. 416p. plates.

524. Strachan, Walter J. The artist and the book in France; the 20th century livre d'artiste. London, Peter Owen, 1969. 368p. illus.

   Glossary includes terms connected with French original bookbinding, p.345-49.

Collections of Plates and Illustrations

525. Abbey, John R. French and Italian collectors and their bindings, illustrated from examples in the library of John Roland Abbey. By A. R. A. Hobson. Oxford, Printed for presentation to the members of the Roxburghe Club, 1953. 190p.

526. Béraldi, Henri. Bibliothèque Henri Béraldi. Paris, Ader, 1934-35. 5 vols. mounted illus. plates.

527. De Ricci, Seymour. French signed bindings in the Mortimer L. Schiff collection. N.Y., 1935. 613p. 336 plates.

528. Derôme, Léopold. La reliure de luxe. Paris, Rouveyre, 1888. 246p. 65 plates.

529. Ledieu, Alcius. Les reliures artistiques et armoriées de la Bibliothèque Communale d'Abbeville. Paris, 1891. 127p. 71 illus. 18 plates.

530. [Morgan, John P.] Armorial bindings from the libraries of the kings and emperors of France from Francis I to Napoleon III. Wittingham, Chiswick Press, 1902. 35 leaves. 33 colored plates.

531. Olivier, Eugène et al. Manuel de l'amateur de reliures armoriées françaises. Paris, 1924-38. 30 vols. illus.

532. Paris, Bibliothèque Nationale. Les plus belles reliures de la réunion des bibliothèques nationales. Paris, Van Oest, 1929. 83p. 16 plates.

General Works

533. Brun, Robert. "Bindings." (In Lejard, André, ed. The art of the French book. London, Elek, 1947. p.141-64)

534. _____. "La reliure." (In Le livre; les plus beaux exemplaires de la Bibliothèque Nationale. Paris, Edition du Chêne, 1942. p.141-64)

535. Calot, Frantz et al. "Bibliophiles et bibliothèques." (In L'art du livre en France. Paris, Librairie Delagrave, 1931. p.264-80)

536. _____. "La reliure." (In L'art du livre en France. Paris, Librairie Delagrave, 1931. p.232-63)

537. Davidson, Louis. "Bookbinding in France to the Revolution." Thesis, Western Reserve Univ., 1957.

538. Devauchelle, Roger. La reliure en France, de ses origines à nos jours. Paris, Rousseau-Girard, 1959-61. 3 vols. plates.

539. Devaux, Yves. Dix siècles de reliure. Paris, Editions Pygmalion, 1977. 398p. illus. 10 leaves of plates.

540. Deville, Etienne. La reliure française. Paris, Van Oest, 1930-31. 2 vols. plates.

541. Fletcher, William Y. Bookbinding in France. N.Y., Macmillan, 1895. 80p. illus.

542. Fournier, Edouard. L'art de la reliure en France aux derniers siècles. Paris, Gay, 1864. 235p. 2d ed., 1888.

543. Grand-Carteret, John. Les almanachs français: bibliographie-- iconographie des almanacs--années--annuaires--calendriers--chansonniers-- étrennes, etc. Paris, Alisie, 1896. 846p. illus.

544. Griesbach, Elsie. "Art of the French bookbinder." Columbia library columns 4:19-27, Nov. 1954.

545. Gruel, Léon. Manuel historique et bibliographique de l'amateur de reliures. Paris, Gruel and Engelmann, 1887-1905. 2 vols. illus. plates. facs.

546. Jacquot, Albert. Essai de répertoire des artistes lorrains; imprimeurs et relieurs. Paris, Plon-Nourrit, 1912. 21p.

547. Lacroix, Paul. "Essai historique sur la reliure en France depuis la seizième siècle." Bulletin du bibliophile 1863, p.611-29.

548. Michel, Marius. La reliure française, commerciale et industrielle depuis l'invention de l'imprimerie jusqu'à nos jours. Paris, Morgan and Fatout, 1881. 137p. illus. plates.

549. _____. La reliure française depuis l'invention de l'imprimerie jusqu'à la fin du xviiie siècle. Paris, 1880. 144p.

550. Michon, Louis M. La reliure française. Paris, Larousse, 1951. 144p. 64 plates.

551. Quentin-Bauchart, Ernest. Les femmes bibliophiles de France. Paris, Morgand, 1886. 2 vols. illus. plates.

552. Toulet, Jean. Introduction à l'histoire de la reliure française XV-XVIIIe siècles. Paris, Bibliothèque Nationale, 1973. 51 leaves. illus.

553. Uzanne, Octave. L'art dans la décoration extérieure des livres en France et à l'étranger. Paris, May, 1898. 272p. illus. plates.

Early History to 1700

554. Austin, Gabriel. The library of Jean Grolier; a preliminary catalog. With an introductory study, "Jean Grolier and the Renaissance" by Colin Eisler. N.Y., Grolier Club, 1971. 137p. illus. facs. plates.

555. Bachelin-Deflorenne, Antoine (Julien, Le bibliophile, pseud.). "Diane de Poitiers." Bibliophile français 1869, p.193-200.

556. British Museum. Bookbindings from the library of Jean Grolier; a loan exhibition 23 Sept.-31 Oct. 1965. London, 1965. 75p. plates.

557. Claudin, Anatole. Les libraires, les reliures, et les imprimeurs de Toulouse au 16e siècle (1531-1550). Paris, 1895. 70p.

558. Clouzot, Henri. Un marché de reliures sous Louis XIII. Paris, Leclerc, 1905. 9p.

559. Dacier, Emile. "Autour de Le Gascon et de Florimond Badier." Les trésors des bibliothèques de France 3:77-90. 1930.

560. _____. "Les premières reliures françaises à décor doré: l'atelier des reliures Louis XII." Les trésors des bibliothèques de France 5:7-40. 1935.

560a. Davenport, Cyril J. Cameo book-stamps figured and described. London, Edward Arnold, 1911. 207p.

560b. Fletcher, William Y. "Florimond Badier." Bibliographica 1:257-61. 1895.

561. _____. "The library of Grolier." Connoisseur 2:14-21, Jan. 1902.

562. Foot, Mirjam M. "Thomas Mahieu, his bindings and his binders." (In The Henry Davis gift: a collection of bindings. London, British Library, 1978. vol. 1, p. 183-91)

563. Fürstenberg, Jean. Le grand siècle en France et ses bibliophiles. Hamburg, Hauswedell, 1972. 160p. and 60 slides of bindings.

564. Gauthier, Marie-Madeleine. "A Limoges champlevé book cover in the
Gambier-Parry collection." Burlington magazine 109:151-57, Mar. 1967.

    An excellent article for general information on Limoges enamel
    bindings between 1170 and 1220 or 1230.

565. _____. Les reliures en émail de Limoges conservées en France:
recensement raisonné." (In Humanisme actif: mélanges d'art et de
littérature offerts à Julien Cain. Paris, Hermann, 1968. vol. 1,
p.271-87)

566. Gruel, Léon. Quelques mots sur les reliures exécutées pour
Marguerite de Valois, reine de France et de Navarre. Paris, Leclerc,
1922. 2, 11, 5p. facs.

    Bound with his Etude sur les Magnus (1922).

567. Harrisse, Henry. Le président de Thou et ses descendants, leur
célèbre bibliothèque. Paris, Leclerc, 1905. 274p. illus.

568. Hobson, Geoffrey D. Maioli, Canevari and others. London, Benn,
1926. 178p. 64 plates.

    Contains information about Thomas Mahieu (Maiolus) and Jean
    Grolier, two 16th century French bibliophiles. Includes new in-
    formation about the ownership of the so-called Canevari bindings.
    (see early history of Italian binding in this bibliography).

569. _____. "Parisian binding, 1500-1525." Library 11:393-434 and
plates, Mar. 1931.

570. _____. Les reliures à la fanfare. 2d ed. Augmentée d'un
supplément contenant des additions et corrections par Anthony R. A.
Hobson. Amsterdam, Van Heusden, 1970. 151, 17p. illus.

571. Kyriss, Ernst. "Pariser Einbände der 2.Hälfte des 16.Jahrhunderts."
Archiv für Geschichte des Buchwesens 10:columns 837-64, 1969/70.

572. Deleted.

573. Lavagne, Xavier. "Répertoire des reliures aux armes des de Thou,
conservées à la bibliothèque Victor-Cousin." Revue française d'histoire
du livre 4:267-98. 1974.

    Jacques A. de Thou (1553-1617) was a French historian, statesman,
    and bibliophile.

574. Leroux de Lincy, Antoine. Researches concerning Jean Grolier, his
life and his library. Rev. and translated by Carolyn Shipman. N.Y.,
Grolier, 1907. 386p. plates. facs.

    Contains a partial catalog of his books.

575. Lesne, Emile. "Ce qui fait le prix des livres: les reliures
précieuse." (In Histoire de la propriété ecclésiastique en France.
Lille, Facultés Catholiques, 1938. vol. 4, p. 6-13)

576. Louisy, Paul. L'ancienne France. Le livre and les arts qui s'y
rattachent. Paris, Librairie de Fermin-Didot, 1887. 271p. illus. facs.

577. Michon, Louis M. "Les reliures exécutées pour François premier."
Gazette des beaux arts 7:309-22, May 1932.

578. _____. "Reliures normandes du début du 16ᵉ siècle." Les trésors
des bibliothèques de France 5:129-39. 1935.

579. Nixon, Howard. "French bookbindings for Sir Richard Wingfield and
Grolier." (In Gatherings in honor of Dorothy E. Miner. Ed. by Ursula
E. McCracken et al. Baltimore, Walters Art Gallery, 1974. p.301-15)

580. _____. "Grolier's binders. Notes on the Paris exhibition."
Book collector 9:45-51, Spring 1960; 9:165-70, Summer 1960.

     Exhibition of the Société de la Reliure Originale in the Biblio-
     thèque Nationale in 1959.

581. Pichon, Jérôme. "Boyet." Bulletin du bibliophile 1906, p.434-38.

582. _____. "Claude de Picques, relieur du roi." Bulletin du bibliophile 1906, p.441-43.

583. _____. "Nicolas Eve." Bulletin du bibliophile 1906, p.439-40.

584. Porcher, J. "Les livres de Diane de Poitiers." Les trésors des
bibliothèques de France 26:78-89, 1942/46.

585. Rondot, Natalis. "Les relieurs de livres à Lyon." Bulletin du
bibliophile 1896, p.285-97.

586. Thierry-Poux, Olgar. Premiers monuments de l'imprimerie en France
au XVᵉ siècle. Paris, Hachette, 1890. 24, 8p. 167 facs on 40 plates.

587. Unterkircher, Franz. "Der Grolier-Einbände der Österreichischen
Nationalbibliothek." Gutenberg Jahrbuch 1959, p.249-58)

18th Century

588. Boinet, Amédée. "Les reliures révolutionnaires." Gutenberg
Jahrbuch 1957, p.339-45.

589. Clouzot, Henri. "La tradition du papier peint en France au 17ᵉ et
18ᵉ siècle." Gazette des beaux arts 7:131-43, Feb. 1912.

590. Comparato, Frank E. "France: la reliure belle." (In his Books
for the millions. Harrisburg, Stackpole, 1971. p.19-40)

591. Dauriac, Jacques P. "Great century of the little almanac. French
book covers." Novum Gebrauchsgraphik 44:44-51, Aug. 1973.

592. Devaux, Yves. "Les ateliers du reliure au xviiiᵉ siècle." Art et
métiers du livre no. 78:8-11, Jan.-Feb. 1978; no. 78:6-9, Mar. 1978.

593. Foot, Mirjam M. "Some eighteenth-century French ateliers." (In
The Henry Davis gift. Collection of bindings. London, British Library,
1978. vol. 1, p.192-206).

594. Fournier, Edouard. [Duseuil] Gazette des beaux arts 16:428-30,
May 1864.

595. Fürstenberger, Hans. "Die Buchbinder, Buchhandler und Buchdrucker."
(In Das französische Buch im achtzehnten Jahrhundert und in der Empirezeit.
Weimar, Gesellschaft der Bibliophilen, 1929. p.163-210)

596. Guiffrey, J. J. "Les grands relieurs parisiens du xviie siècle:
Boyet, Padeloup, Derôme." Bulletin de la Société de L'Histoire de Paris
11:98-112. 1884.

597. Helwig, Hellmuth. "Derôme, eine Pariser Buchbinderfamilie des 17/18
Jahrhunderts." Allgemeiner Anzeiger für Buchbinderein 73:174-78. 1960.

598. Husung, Max J. "Padeloup der Jüngere...." Archiv für Buchbinderei
31:29-31. 1931.

    About Antoine-Michel Padeloup (1685-1758).

599. Ludwigsburg. Castle. Das Buch als Kunstwerk; französische illus-
trierte Bücher des 18. Jahrhunderts aus der Bibliothek Hans Fürstenberg.
[Catalog by Werner R. Deusch] Ludwigsburg, 1965. 161p. 144 illus.

600. Michon, Louis M. "Notes sur les reliures de l'atelier des Monnier."
(In Mélanges d'histoire littéraire à Jean Bonnerot.... Paris, Librairie
Nizet, 1954. p.509-13)

601. Mornand, Pierre. Le livre et sa reliure aux xviie et xviiie siècles.
Paris, Editions Elzevir, 1942? 16p.

602. Ramsden, Charles. "French bookbinding 1789-1849." Library
5:258-60, Mar. 1951.

603. "Les reliures en mosaïques du xviiie siècle." Gazette des beaux
arts 20:358-65, Oct. 1879.

604. Le siècle d'or de l'imprimerie lyonnaise. Réd. by Henri Hours
et al. Paris, Editions du Chêne, 1972. 162p. plates (some in color).

    Contains an essay on binding in Lyon by Jean Toulet.

605. Uzanne, Octave. The French bookbinders of the eighteenth century.
Chicago, Caxton Club, 1904. 133p. illus. 20 plates.

19th Century

606. Art Journal. The Crystal Palace Exhibition illustrated catalog,
London 1851; an unabridged republication of the Art Journal special issue.
With a new introduction by John Gloag. N.Y., Dover, 1970. 328, 62p.

    Contains 3 illustrations of bindings by Madame Gruel.

607. Belville, Eugène. "L'exposition de la reliure moderne au Musée
Galleria." L'art décoratif no. 47:191-99, Aug. 1902.

    Contains illustrations of bindings by Marius Michel, Canapé, Cuzin,
    Ruban, and Belville. For René Kieffer 7 illustrations are given,
    including 2 endpapers.

608. Carteret, Léopold. "Reliures romantique et cartonnages mosaïqués."
(In Le trésor du bibliophile romantique et moderne 1801-1875. Paris,
1927. vol. 3, p.15-18)

609. "Catalogue of books bequeathed to the New York Public Library by
William Augustus Spencer." Bulletin of the New York Public Library
18:540-72, June 1914.

    Contains index of binders and titles of their books, p.570-72.
    Illustrations of bindings by Lortic, Gruel, and Marius Michel.

610. Charpentier, Thérèse. "Un aspect peu connu de l'activité de
Lautrec: sa collaboration à la reliure d'art." Gazette des beaux arts
56:165-78, Sept. 1960.

    Toulouse-Lautrec furnished the cartoons and René Wiener of Nancy
    did the binding.

611. Cluzel, Etienne. "Sur le relieur Thouvenin." Bulletin du bibliophile 1948, p.348-55.

    About Joseph Thouvenin (1790-1834). Contains a reprint of article
    about the binder by Jules Janin, which appeared in vol. 6, Jan. 18,
    1834, of L'artiste.

612. Culot, Paul. Jean Claude Bozérian: un monument de l'ornement dans
la reliure de France. Brussels, Speeckaert, 1979. 107p.

613. Devauchelle, Roger. "Joseph Thouvenin dit Thouvenin l'aîné."
Le livre et l'estampe 1958, p.156-66.

614. Ehrman, Albert. "Les relieurs vernis sans odeur, autrement dit
'vernis martin'." Book collector 14:523-27, winter 1965; 15:351-52. 1966.

615. Foulon, Maurice. Eugène Varlin, relieur et membre de la Commune.
Clermont-Ferrand, Editions Mont-Louis, 1934. 244p.

616. "French bookbinding 1789-1848; summary of a paper by Mr. Charles
Ramsden [read before the Bibliographical Society, Dec. 19, 1950]"
Library 5:258-60, Mar. 1951.

617. Girard, Henri. "Le livre, l'illustration et la reliure à l'époque
romantique." (In Le romantique et l'art. Paris, Laurens, 1928.
p.288-317)

618. Giraud, Jean B. Lucien Magnin, relieur lyonnais, 1849-1903. Lyon,
Rey and Cie, 1905. 36p. 80 plates.

619. Gruel, Léon. Reliures en vernis sans odeur. Paris, Leclerc, 1900.
12p. illus.

    Extract from Bulletin du bibliophile 1900, p.187-94.

620. _____. "Le style à la fin du xix^a siècle dans les arts décoratifs appliqués à la reliure des livres." Bulletin du bibliophile 1896,
p.66-73.

621. _____. "Les Thouvenin." Bulletin du bibliophile 1898,
p.435-46, 508-14.

622. Herscher, E. "Petit essai sur les cartonnages de l'époque
romantique." Arts et métiers graphiques no. 18:999-1004, July 15, 1930.

623. Kent, Henry W. "The Spencer collection of modern bookbindings."
Bulletin of the New York Public Library 18:533-38, June 1914.

    Contains illustrations of bindings by Cuzin, Mercier, and Canapé.
    William A. Spencer (died 1912) was a wealthy American who lived in
    Paris and accumulated a distinguished collection of 19th century
    bindings and illustrations, chiefly French. He willed his library
    to the New York Public.

624. Meier-Graefe, A. J. "Some recent continental bookbindings."
Studio 9:37-50, Oct. 1895.

625. Nodier, Charles. "De la reliure en France au 19^a siècle."
Bulletin du bibliophile 18:241-50. 1939.

626. "Painting and the graphic arts." (In Art nouveau, Belgium, France.
Catalogue of an exhibition organized by the Institute for the Arts, Rice
University and the Art Institute of Chicago. By Yvonne Brunhammer et al.
Houston, Institute for the Arts, Rice University, 1976. p.40-93)

627. Pichon, Jérôme. "Antoine Bauzonnet." Bulletin du bibliophile
1906, p.426-34.

628. Prideaux, Sarah T. "Modern French binding." (In Modern bookbindings their design and decoration. London, Constable, 1906. p.59-104)

629. Roethel, Michel. "Les cartonnages Hetzel." Connaissances des arts
no. 314:97-105, April 1978.

    Contains many illustrations in color of Jules Verne's books with
    their very attractive covers. Pierre-Jules Hetzel (1814-) was
    an editor and publisher in Paris.

630. Roylance, Dale. "The Altschul collection: the arts of the French
book 1838-1967." Yale University library gazette 44, no. 2:47-102, Oct.
1969.

    Binder's name is given for each title in collection. List of
    binders, p.100-01. Many books bound by Mercier and Lucie Weill.

631. Saunier, Charles. "La reliure moderne." L'art décoratif no. 30:
253-63, Mar. 1901.

Most of the article is on French binders: Marius Michel, Ruban,
Canapé, Mme Antoinette Vallgren, Eugène Belville, and Pierre Roche.

632. Thévenin, Léon. "Opinion sur la reliure moderne. Etude sur
Charles Meunier." Mercure de France 108:514-24. 1914.

633. Uzanne, Octave. "French bookbindings." Studio, special winter
no. 1899-1900, p.57-66.

20th Century

634. Ackerman, Phyllis. "Modernism in bookbinding." International
studio 80:145-49, Nov. 1924.

Contains illustrations of bindings by Legrain and René Kieffer.

635. Abbey, John R. An exhibition of modern English and French bindings
from the collection of Major J. R. Abbey. London, Arts Council, 1949.
30p. plates.

636. Baschet, Roger. "Henri Mercher: un technicien certes, mais aussi
un novateur." Art et métiers du livre no. 76, p.8-11, Oct.-Nov. 1977.

637. Beuchler, André. "Présentation du livre." Art et décoration
no. 16:27-31. 1950.

Contains many illustrations of book covers, including two by
Paul Bonet.

638. Blaizot, Georges. Masterpieces of French modern bindings. N.Y.,
Services Culturels Français, 1947. 128p. illus. (some in color)

Most of the illustrations are for Pierre Legrain and Paul Bonet.
Contains information about Jean Dunand (1877-1942), a Swiss artist
in Paris, who did remarkable lacquer work for bindings.

639. Brugalla, Emilio. La encuadernacion en Paris en las avanzadas del
arte moderno. Barcelona, Asociacion de Bibliofilos Barcelona, 1954.
91p. plates (in portfolio)

640. California Palace of the Legion of Honor, San Francisco. French
art of the book. San Francisco, 1949. 48p. illus. (exhibit catalog)

641. "Catalogue des reliures de Monique Mathieu." Bulletin du
bibliophile 1973, p.128-46, 271-96.

642. Chambre Syndicale Du Livre d'Amateur, Paris. Livres illustrés
français et reliures d'art de 1940 à 1950. Paris, 1950? 39p. 40 plates
(exhibit catalog)

643. Chavance, René. "Les reliures d'Alfred Latour." Art et décoration
62:175-80, June 1933.

644. Crauzat, Ernest de. La reliure française de 1900 à 1925. Paris, 1932. 2 vols. 395 plates (500 reproductions)

645. Dally, Ph. "Les techniques modernes de la reliure." Art et décoration 51:15-24. 1927.

     Contains illustrations of bindings by Rose Adler, Jeanne Langrand, Geneviève de Léotard, Madeleine Gras, Legrain, Germaine Schroeder, and Marguerite Bernard.

646. Deshairs, Léon. "Robert Bonfils." Art et décoration 55:33-43. 1929.

     Contains illustrations for 4 bindings. Two more bindings are in Studio 89:229, April 1925.

647. Dormoy, Marie. Jacques Doucet. Abbeville, 1931. 29p.

     Jacques Doucet (1853-1929) was a French couturier, book collector, and patron of the arts. Pierre Legrain designed many bindings for him.

648. Farnoux-Reynaud, Lucien. "La reliure d'art, triomphe du goût français." Mobilier et décoration, Feb. 1938, p.58-78.

649. Gaigneron, Axelle de. "Cet art discret, la reliure." Connaissance des arts no. 305:62-69, July 1977.

     Contains illustrations of bindings by Daniel Mercer, Paul Ameline, Georges Leroux, Jean-Paul Miguet, Henri Mercher, Claude Honnaître, Monique Mathieu, Alain Lobstein, Alain Devauchelle, Claude Delpierre, and Kirsten Vinding.

650. Garvey, Eleanor M. and Wick, Peter A. The arts of the French book 1900-1965. Dallas, Southern Methodist Univ. Press, 1967. 119p. illus.

     Contains brief descriptions of bindings by Henri Creuzevault, Madeleine Gras, Marius Michel et al.

651. Great Britain. Arts Council. Modern French bookbindings by members of the Société de la Reliure Originale. London, 1961. 27p. illus. (exhibit catalog)

652. Joubin, André. "Jacques Doucet 1853-1929." Gazette des beaux arts, Feb. 1930, p.69-82.

653. Karlikow, Abe. "Bookbinding by Alice and Georges Leroux." Craft horizons 22:32-35, Mar. 1962.

654. Lada-Mocarski, Polly. "New French onlay; a French binder seeks freedom from restrictions of an old technique." Craft horizons 18:38-39, Jan. 1958.

     About Claude Stahly.

655. _____ and Karlikow, Abe. "Conversation with Pierre Martin,
master binder." Craft horizons 21:15-17, May 1961.

656. _____ and Lyon, Mary. "Bookbinding: the art of Mary Reynolds."
Craft horizons 21:11-13, Jan. 1961.

   Mary Reynolds was an American binder who spent 30 years of her
   life in Paris.

657. Legrain, Pierre. Pierre Legrain relieur: répertoire descriptif
et bibliographique de mille deux cent trente-six reliures...243 reproductions en héliogravure et 7 planches en couleurs. Paris, Blaizot, 1965.
204p. 7 colored plates, 72 numb. plates on 36 leaves.

   Contains a biographical sketch by Jacques Antoine-Legrain,
   "Souvenirs sur Pierre Legrain."

658. Lièvre, P. "Pierre Legrain." Plaisir de bibliophile 3:130-44.
1927.

659. "Un maître de la reliure d'art: Rose Adler." Art et décoration
no. 73:46-47, May 1959.

660. Marcilhac, Félix. "New ideas in French bookbinding 1914-1939."
Bulletin of the Decorative Arts Society (U.K.) 1:36-43. 1976.
(unverified)

661. Moutard-Uldry, Renée. "La reliure française contemporaine."
Visage du monde no. 95:17-21. 1950.

662. N. Y. Museum of Contemporary Crafts. La reliure originale française.
Bookbindings by contemporary French binders. Organized under the patron-
age of the Société de la Reliure Originale. N.Y., 1964. 52p. illus.

   Gives descriptions of 142 books by contemporary French binders:
   Jacqueline Antona, Paul Bonet, Robert Bonfils, Georges Cretté,
   Germaine de Coster and Hélène Dumas, Roger Devauchelle, Georges
   Leroux, Alain Lobstein, Pierre-Lucien Martin, Monique Mathieu,
   Henri Mercher, and Claude Stahly.

663. Paris. Bibliothèque Nationale. Reliures: Monique Mathieu, Georges
Leroux, Jean de Gonet Paris, 1978. 68p. illus. (exhibit catalog)

664. Peignot, Jérome. "Le luxe 1925 du livre relié." Connaissance des
arts no. 277:100-05, March 1975.

   Contains bindings by Georges Cretté, Gruel, François-Louis Schmied,
   and Jean Dunand.

665. Preston, Emily. "Modern tendencies in bookbinding." Independent
69:1266-71, Dec. 8, 1910.

666. Prideaux, Sarah T. "French binders of today." Scribner's magazine
19:361-70, Mar. 1896.

667. Deleted.

668. Rosenthal, Leon. "Pierre Legrain, relieur." Art et décoration
43:65-70. 1923.

669. Roylance, Dale. "The Altschul collection: the arts of the French
book 1838-1967." Yale University library gazette 44:47-102, Oct. 1969.

670. Société de la Reliure Originale. Exposition...accompagnée d'une
présentation de reliures ayant appartenu à Jean Grolier. Paris, 1959.
150p. plates.

  Exhibition at the Bibliothèque Nationale. Contains Jacques
  Guignard's "Jean Grolier et la reliure française au xvie siècle,"
  p.xv-xxvii. Includes bindings by Rose Adler, Paul Bonet, Robert
  Bonfils, Georges Cretté, Jean Knoll, Pierre-Lucien Martin, and
  others.

671. _____. Exposition de la Société...pour le xxe anniversaire de
sa fondation. Paris, 1965. 114p. 31 plates.

672. Société des Bibliophiles et Iconophiles de Belgique. Reliures du
xxe siècle. De Marius Michel à Paul Bonet. Exposition à la Bibliothèque
Royale de Belgique. By Franz Schauwers and Georges Colin. Brussels, 1957.
84p. 27 plates.

673. Sotheby and Co. Catalog of fine modern French and German illustrated books and bindings. London, 1970. 124p. illus. plates.

674. Strachan, Walter J. "Art binding." (In The artist and the book
in France. London, Peter Owen, 1969. p.274-87)

675. Taylor, E. A. "The art of the book in France." (In Holme,
Charles, ed. The art of the book. London, Studio, 1914. p.179-200)

  Contains 3 illustrations of parchment and vellum bindings by
  André Mare, who tooled and colored them.

676. Thornton, Lynne. "Contemporary crafts in France." Connoisseur
no. 206:229-33, Mar. 1981.

  Contains a brief description of the cooperative work of Germaine
  de Coster and Hélène Dumas. They are known for their sumptuous
  bindings.

677. Valéry, Paul et al. Paul Bonet. Paris, Blaizot, 1945. 259p.
plates.

Germany

Reference Works

678. Davies, Hugh W.,ed. Catalogue of early German books of C. Fairfax
Murray. London, Holland Press, 1961. 2 vols. illus.

  Reprint of 1913 ed. Includes imprints from Germany, Holland,
  Belgium, and Switzerland for the years 1460-1680.

679. Helwig, Hellmuth. Das deutsche Buchbinder-Handwerk; Handwerks- und Kulturgeschichte. Stuttgart, Hiersemann, 1962-65. 2 vols.

General Works

680. Davenport, Cyril J. "Bookbinding in Germany." Library Association record 12:49-51, Feb. 15, 1910.

681. Mitchell, William S. "Some German bindings in Aberdeen University Library." (In Festschrift Ernst Kyriss. Stuttgart, Hettler, 1961. p.175-90)

682. Pfaff, Otto, ed. Buch und Bucheinbände; eine Werbeschrift. Halle/Salle, Knapp, 1926. 46p. plates.

683. Rhein, Adolf. Erfurter Buchbinder seit 500 Jahren. Erfurt, 1937. 63p. illus.

Early History to 1800

684. Bollert, Martin. Lederschnittbände des xiv Jahrhunderts. Leipzig, 1925. 77p. 36 plates.

685. Geck, E. "Verzeichnis der Mainzer Buchbinder." Mainzer Zeitschrift 67/68:60-67. 1972/73.

686. Geldner, Ferdinand. Bamberger und Nürnberger Lederschnittbände. Munich, Zink, 1953. 58p. 13 plates.

687. _____. "Bekannte und unbekannte bayerische Klosterbuchbinderein der spätgotischen Zeit." Archiv für Geschichte des Buchwesens 2:154-60. 1960.

688. Goff, Frederick R. "Fifteenth century stamped bindings from the Benedictine monastery of St. Peter at Erfurt." Gutenberg Jahrbuch 1969, p.274-79.

689. Haebler, Konrad. Rollen- und Plattenstempel des xvi Jahrhunderts. Leipzig, Harrassowitz, 1928-29. 2 vols.

690. Helwig, Hellmuth. "Deutsche Klosterbuchbinderein: eine Übersicht." Archiv für Geschichte des Buchwesens 4:225-84. 1963.

691. Hobson, Geoffrey D. "German Renaissance patrons of bookbinding." Book collector 3:171-84, autumn 1954; 3:251-71, winter 1954.

    Second article has information on the book collecting activities of several members of the Fugger family: Raimondo (1489-1535); John Jacob, his son and a greater bibliophile; Marcus (1529-97), the greatest; and Philip Edward (1546-1618).

692. Knaus, Hermann. "Deutsche Stempelbände des 13. Jahrhunderts." Gutenberg Jahrbuch 1963, p.245-53.

693. Kyriss, Ernst. "An Esslingen binder of the late Gothic period."
Speculum 25:73-77, Jan. 1950.

694. _____. "Johannes Zoll, ein Tübinger Buchbinder des 15. Jahrhunderts." (In Aus der Welt des Buches. Festgabe zum 70. Geburtstag von
Georg Leyh. Leipzig, Harrassowitz, 1950. p.84-93)

695. _____. "Notes on Nuremburg panel stamps before the Reformation."
Publications of the Bibliographical Society of America 44:59-62, 1st
quarter 1950.

696. _____. "Nürnberger Klostereinbände der Jahre 1433 bis 1525."
Dissertation, Univ. of Erlangen, 1940. 87p. illus.

      Published by Reinde in Bamberg in 1940.

697. _____. "Stuttgarter Buchbinder der Renaissancezeit 1540-1630."
Zeitschrift für Bibliothekswesen 67:173-91. 1953.

698. _____. Verzierte gotische Einbände im alten deutschen
Sprachgebiet. Stuttgart, Hettler, 1951-58. 4 vols. plates.

699. Layer, Adolf. "Der Augsburger Buchbinder Johann Georg Mozart."
Archiv für Geschichte des Buchwesens 11:columns 873-84. 1970.

700. Lehmann, Paul J. Eine Geschichte der alten Fuggerbibliotheken.
Tübingen, Mohr, 1956-60. 2 vols. illus. plates.

701. Leskien, Elfriede. "Spätgotische Einbände aus dem Rheingebiet."
(In Festschrift Ernst Kyriss. Stuttgart, Hettler, 1961. p.149-58)

702. Loubier, Jean. "Johann Richenbachs Bucheinbände." Zeitschrift für
Bibliothekswesen 29:19-25. 1912. 35:128-33. 1918.

703. Mitius, Otto. Fränkische Lederschnittbände des xv Jahrhunderts.
Leipzig, Haupt, 1909. 44p. 13 plates.

704. Pingrée, Isabelle. "Richenbach bindings in the United States."
Gutenberg Jahrbuch 1977, p.330-44.

705. Rest, Josef. "Neues über Johannes Richenbach." Jahrbuch der
Einbandkunst 2:47-59. 1928.

706. Ricci, Seymour de. "Jean Richenbach: un relieur du xve siècle."
Zentralblatt für Bibliothekswesen 27:409-12. 1910.

707. Rohde, H. P. "Storhandel og bibliofili. En bogbindshistorisk
studie." Bogvennen 10:21-50. 1955.

708. Schmidt, Christel. Jakob Krause. Leipzig, Hiersemann, 1923.
83p. illus. facs.

709. Schramm, Percy E. and Mütherich, Florentine. Denkmale der deutschen
Könige und Kaiser...768-1250. Munich, Prestel, 1962. 484p.

      Contains descriptions and plates for several book covers.

710. Schreiber, Heinrich. "Adolar Baldensheym, ein Leipziger Renaissance-
buchbinder." (In Beiträge zum Rollen- und Platteneinband im 16. Jahrhundert. Ed. by Ilse Schunke. Leipzig, Harrassowitz, 1937. p.176-200)

711. _____. "Die alten Einbände der Gutenberg-Bibel." Zentralblatt
für Bibliothekswesen 57:511-23. 1940.

712. _____. Augsburger Buchbinder der Gotik und Renaissance.
Stuttgart, Hettler, 1938. 19p. illus.

713. _____. "Der Kölner Rollen- und Platteneinband im 16. Jahrhundert." (In Beiträge zum Rollen- und Platteneinband im 16. Jahrhundert.
Ed. by Ilse Schunke. Leipzig, Harrassowitz, 1937. p.311-97)

714. _____. "Deutsche Einbände der Gegenreformation." Gutenberg
Jahrbuch 47:363-72. 1972.

715. _____. "Die romanischen Einbände in Deutschland." (In
Festschrift Ernst Kyriss. Stuttgart, Hettler, 1961. p.17-32)

716. _____. Jakob Krause. Stuttgart, Hettler, 1953. 79p. illus.
plates.

717. _____. Leben und Werk Jakob Krauses. Leipzig, Insel-Verlag,
1943. 150p. illus. plates.

718. _____. Studien zum Bilderschmuck der deutschen Renaissance-
Einbände. Wiesbaden, Harrassowitz, 1959. 151p. illus.

719. Theele, Joseph. Die Handschriften des Benediktinerklosters S. Petri
zu Erfurt. Leipzig, Harrassowitz, 1920. 220p. 2 plates.

     Contains an essay on the monastery's bindery by Paul Schwenke.

19th Century

720. Comparato, Frank E. "Germany: die schöne Borse." (In Books for
the millions. Harrisburg, Pa., Stackpole, 1971. p.73-95)

721. Grautoff, Otto. Die Entwicklung der modernen Buchkunst in
Deutschland. Leipzig, Seemann, 1901. 219p. illus.

722. _____. "Der modernen künstlerisches Handeinband in Deutschland."
Zeitschrift für Bücherfreunde 7:49-76. 1903/4.

723. Harms, Bernhard. Zur Entwicklungsgeschichte der deutschen Buchbinderei in der zweiten Hälfte des 19. Jahrunderts. Tübingen, Mohr,
1902. 184p.

724. Maul, Johannes und Friedel, Hans. Deutsche Bucheinbände der
Neuzeit. Leipzig, 1888. 42 colored plates in portfolio.

20th Century

725. Bogeng, Gustav A. Deutsche Einbandkunst im ersten Jahrzehnt des
zwanzigsten Jahrhunderts. Halle, 1911. xxiiip. 78 plates.

726. _____. "Neue Einbände von Paul Kersten." Archiv für Buchbinderei
14, no. 2:19-24. 1914.

727. Collin, Ernst. Paul Kersten. Berlin, 1925. 81p. plates.

728. Dannhorn, Hans. "Franz Weisse." Archiv für Buchbinderei 31:1-6.
1931.

729. Deubner, L. "The art of the book in Germany." (In Holme, Charles,
ed. The art of the book. London, Studio, 1914. p.127-76)

730. Eckhardt, Wolfgang. Otto Dorfner. Stuttgart, Hettler, 1960. 39p.
illus.

731. Festschrift Hübel & Denck, Leipzig, 1875-1925. Leipzig, 1925.
141p. plates.

732. Glauning, Otto. "Newest developments in bookbinding." Archiv für
Buchgewerbe 65:99-132. 1940.

733. Göpel, Erhard. Der Buchbinder Ignatz Wiemeler. Brunn, Rohrer,
1938. 24p. illus.

734. Grautoff, Otto. "Der moderne Künstlerische Handeinband in
Deutschland." Zeitschrift für Bücherfreunde 7:49-76. 1903/1904.

735. Greeven, E. A. Die Buchbinder Gerbers in Hamburg 1830-1955.
Hamburg, 1955. 55p.

736. Hager, Victor. "Bruno Scheer." Buch und Schrift 10:177-79. 1937.

737. Halbey, Hans. "Bookbinding by Kurt Londenberg." Craft horizons
27:30-33, Jan. 1967.

738. Herbst, Hermann. Tider Woltmann, ein Braunschweiger Buchbinder des
15.Jahrhunderts. Braunschweig, Appelhans, 1938. 39p. 12 plates.

739. Hofmann, Herbert. "Bookbindings by Otto Pfaff." Deutsche Kunst
und Dekoration 63:224-27, Dec. 1928.

740. _____. "Otto Pfaff." Jahrbuch der Einbandkunst 2:206-12. 1928.

741. Krinitz, Fritz. Frieda Thiersch und ihre Handbuchbinderei.
Stuttgart, 1968. 72p. plates.

742. Lang, Lothar. Expressionist book illustration in Germany 1907-1927.
Translated by Janet Seligman. London, Thames and Hudson, 1976. 246p.
illus.

743. Mágr, Anton S. "Bucheinbände von Carl Sonntag jun." Zeitschrift
für Bücherfreunde 1:36-40. 1909/10.

744. Meyer, J. J. de L. "Fine binding as a contemporary art." Penrose annual 58:237-48, 1965.

745. Moderne Einbandgestaltung und Ignatz Wiemeler. Internationales Symposium 11/12 Sept. 1972 in Gewerbemuseum Basel. Redigiert von A. Cizinsky und W. Jägge. Bern, Schweizerisches Gutenberg Museum, 1972. 120p.

746. Deleted.

747. "Neue Bucheinbände und Leder-arbeiten." Deutsche Kunst und Dekoration 67:348-53, Feb. 1931.

748. N. Y. Museum of Modern Art. Ignatz Wiemeler, modern bookbinder, Oct. 2d to Oct. 24th, 1935. N.Y., 1935. 16p. illus.

        Contains "Ideals in bookbinding" by Ignatz Wiemeler.

749. Pazaurek, Gustav E. "Otto Dorfners Kunsteinbände." Jahrbuch der Einbandkunst 2:202-05. 1928.

750. Schauer, Georg K. Deutsche Buchkunst 1890 bis 1960. Hamburg, Maximilian-Gesellschaft, 1963. 2 vols. illus. plates.

        Excellent bibliography in vol. 2, p.2-32; remainder of volume has 163 plates, including many illustrations of bindings.

751. _____. "Kurt Londenberg--Handwerk und Kunst." Philobiblon 1: 118-21, May 1957.

752. _____. "Zum Werk von Emil Rudolf Weiss." Imprimatur 6:146-51. 1969.

753. Sotheby and Co. Catalog of fine modern French and German illustrated books and bindings. London, 1970. 124p. illus. plates.

754. Uzanne, Octave. "Paul Kersten's decorative leather work." International studio 15:112-17, Dec. 1901.

Great Britain

Reference Works

755. Duff, Edward G. A century of the English book trade; short notices of all printers, stationers, book-binders, and others connected with it from the issue of the first dated book in 1457 to the incorporation of the Company of Stationers in 1557. London, Blades, East and Blades, 1905. 200p.

756. Herbert, Arthur S. Historical catalogue of printed editions of the English Bible 1525-1961. Rev. and expanded from the edition of T. H. Darlow and H. F. Moule, 1903. London, British and Foreign Bible Society, 1968. 549p.

Brief description of binding for some of the editions. Index has entries for contemporary, embroidered, goffered edges, inlaid leather, royal arms, etc.

757. Howe, Ellic. A list of London bookbinders 1648-1815. London, Bibliographical Society, 1950. 105p.

758. Maxted, Ian. The London book trades 1775-1800; a preliminary checklist of members. Kent, Dawson, 1977. 257p.

759. Nixon, Howard M. Five centuries of English bookbinding. London, Scolar Press, 1978. 232p. and index. 100 plates.

Contains an excellent bibliography, p.225-32.

760. Pollard, Graham. "Names of some English fifteenth-century binders." Library 25:193-218, Sept. 1970.

761. Ramsden, Charles. Bookbinders of the United Kingdom (outside London) 1780-1840. London, 1954. 250p. plates.

762. _____. London bookbinders 1780-1840. London, Batsford, 1956. 155p. plates.

Collections of Plates and Illustrations

763. Abbey, John R. English bindings 1490-1940, in the library of J. R. Abbey. Ed. by Geoffrey D. Hobson. London, Priv. printed at the Chiswick Press, 1940. 201p. plates.

764. Almack, Edward. Fine old bindings in Edward Almack's library. London, Blades, East and Blades, 1913. 149p. plates.

765. Davenport, Cyril J. Royal English bookbindings. London, Seeley, 1896. 95p. plates.

766. Fletcher, William Y. English bookbindings in the British Museum; Illustrations of sixty-three examples selected on account of their beauty or historical interest, with introduction and descriptions by William Y. Fletcher. London, Paul, Trench, Trübner, 1895. 65 leaves. 66 colored plates.

767. Hobson, Geoffrey D. Bindings in Cambridge libraries; seventy-two plates with notes. Cambridge, Univ. Press, 1929. 179p. 72 plates.

768. Maggs Bros., London. Bookbindings of Great Britain, sixteenth to the twentieth century. London, 1957. 157p. illus. (catalog 845)

769. _____. Bookbinding in Great Britain, sixteenth to the twentieth century. London, 1964. 193p. plates. (catalog 893)

770. _____. Bookbindings in Great Britain 16-20 centuries. London, 1975. 292p. illus. (catalog 966)

771. Maggs Bros., London. English armorial and decorative bindings.
London, 1938. 128p. illus. (catalog 665)

772. Moss, William E. Bindings from the library of Robert Dudley, Earl
of Leicester, K.G., 1533-1588; a new contribution to the history of
English sixteenth century gold-tooled bookbindings. Sonning-on-Thames,
1934. 40p. 18 mounted plates.

773. Oldham, James B. Shrewsbury School Library bindings. Oxford,
Printed for the Librarian of the Schrewsbury School at the Univ. Press,
1943. 183p. 62 plates.

     The Library dates back to the end of the 16th century.

774. Quaritch, Bernard. Catalogue of English and foreign bookbindings
offered for sale. London, 1921. 76p. 79 plates.

775. Schiff, Mortimer L. British and miscellaneous signed bindings in
the Mortimer L. Schiff collection. By Seymour de Ricci. N.Y., 1935.
161p. illus. plates.

776. Windsor Castle. Royal Library. Specimens of royal fine and
historical bookbinding selected from the Royal Library, Windsor Castle.
With an introduction and notes by R. R. Holmes. London, Griggs, 1893.
152 plates.

Heraldic Bookstamps

777. Clements, H. J. B. "Armorial bookstamps and their owners."
Library 20:121-35, Sept. 1939.

     Contains two pages of corrections to Davenport's English heraldic
     book-stamps (1909).

778. _____. "Checklist of English armorial book-stamps." Book
collector's quarterly 14:64-72, Apr.-June 1934; 15:68-78, 64-72, July-
Sept., Oct.-Dec. 1934; 16:64-72, Apr.-June 1935; 17:36-46, Apr.-June 1935.

779. Davenport, Cyril J. English heraldic book-stamps. London,
Constable, 1909. 450p. illus.

     See corrections in Library 20:121-35, Sept. 1939.

780. Fletcher, William Y. "English armorial bookstamps and their
owners." Bibliographica 3:309-43. 1897.

781. Pollard, Alfred W. "The Franks collection of armorial bookstamps."
Library 3:115-34, Apr. 1902.

782. Woodfield, Denis. An ordinary of British armorial bookbindings in
the Clements Collection, Victoria and Albert Museum. London, Victoria
and Albert Museum, 1958 (or more probably 1960). 192p. (typescript)
(unverified)

General Works

783. "Armorial bindings: the Clements collection." Times literary supplement, Sept. 14, 1940, p.476.

     Henry John Beresford Clements gave his collection of 1,150 British armorial bindings to the Victoria and Albert Museum in London.

784. Bonnell, Alice H. "Tooled in blind and gold; some British bindings at Columbia." Columbia library columns 20:27-42, May 1971.

785. Bushnell, George H. "Scottish bookbindings and bookbinders 1450-1800." Bookman's journal 15:67-87. 1927.

786. Cook, Davidson. "Illustrations on bindings." Times literary supplement, April 17, 1937, p.296.

787. Davenport, Cyril J. "Bookbinding in England." Library Association record 9:19-23, Jan. 15, 1907.

788. _____ . English embroidered bookbindings. London, Paul, Trench, Trübner, 1899. 113p. illus. 52 plates.

789. _____ . "Gold-tooled binding in England." Bookman's journal and print collector 5:4-7, Oct. 1921.

790. Dean, John F. "English language bookbinding manuals in the context of the history of English bookbinding." Ph.D. dissertation, Graduate Library School, Univ. of Chicago, 1975.

791. Duff, Edward G. "Scottish bookbinding, armorial and artistic." Trans. of the Bibliographical Society 15:95-113. 1918.

792. Fletcher, William Y. Bookbinding in England and France. London, Seeley, 1897. 51, 80p. illus. plates.

793. Kendrick, Albert F. [Embroidered bookbindings] (In English embroidery. London, Newnes, 1904. p.48, 65, 71-72, 75, 91)

794. Middleton, Bernard C. A history of English craft bookbinding technique. N.Y., Hafner, 1963. 307p. illus.

795. Munby, Alan N. "Collecting English signed bindings." Book collector 2:177-93, autumn 1953.

796. Nixon, Howard M. Five centuries of English bookbinding. London Scolar Press, 1978. 232p. and index. 100 plates.

     "I have updated and amended the original Book Collector articles where appropriate."--Introduction, p.9.

797. O'Lochlainn, Colm. "Bookbinding in Ireland." Gutenberg Jahrbuch 11:229-32. 1936.

798. Pollard, Graham. "Changes in the style of bookbinding 1550-1830." Library 11:71-94, June 1956.

799. Sullivan, Edward S. Decorative bookbinding in Ireland. Letchworth, Arden Press, 1914. 34p.

800. Wakeman, Geoffrey. English marbled papers: a documentary history. Loughborough, Plough Press, 1980? 27p. 26 leaves of plates.

Early History to 1600

801. Baker, Carroll M. "Bookbinding and bookbinders in London 1403-1603; a survey of the legal, economic, and social status." Master's thesis, Univ. of Chicago, 1957. 98p.

802. Barker, Nicolas. "Quiring and the binder: quire marks in some meanuscripts in fifteenth century blind-stamped bindings." (In Studies in the book trade in honour of Graham Pollard. Oxford, Bibliographical Society, 1975. p.11-32)

803. Davenport, Cyril J. Thomas Berthelet, royal printer and bookbinder to Henry VIII, King of England. Chicago, Caxton Club, 1901. 102p. illus. plates.

804. Doughty, D. W. "Notes on the Regent Moray's books and their bindings." Bibliothek 6:65-75. 1972.

       Books belonging to Lord James Steuard or Steward, son of King
       James V, Commendator Prior of the Augustine Priory at St. Andrews,
       and better known as the Regent Moray. Bindings were done in France.

805. Duff, Edward G. "The bindings of Thomas Wotton." Library 1:337-47, Oct. 1910.

       Thomas Wotton (1521-87) was a patron of learning and a bibliophile.

806. _____ . The English provincial printers, stationers and book-binders to 1557. Cambridge, Univ. Press, 1912. 153p.

807. _____ . Printers, stationers and bookbinders of London and Westminster in the 15th century. Aberdeen, 1899. 105p.

808. _____ . Printers, stationers and bookbinders of Westminster and London from 1476 to 1535. Cambridge, Univ. Press, 1906. 256p.

809. _____ . "Some early Scottish bookbindings and collectors." Scottish historical review 4:430-42, July 1907.

810. Foot, Mirjam M. "Thomas Wotton and his binders." (In The Henry Davis gift. A collection of bindings. London, British Library, 1978. vol. 1, p.139-55)

811. Gibson, Strickland. Abstracts from the wills and testamentary documents of binders, printers, and stationers of Oxford, from 1493 to 1638. London, Printed for the Bibliographical Society by Blades, East and Blades, 1907. 61p.

812. _____ . Early Oxford bindings. Oxford, Oxford Univ. Press, 1903. 69p. illus.

813. Gray, George J. The earlier Cambridge stationers and bookbinders, and the first Cambridge printer. Oxford, Printed for the Bibliographical Society at the Oxford Univ. Press, 1904. 73p. and plates.

814. Hobson, Geoffrey D. Blind-stamp panels in the English book trade, c.1485-1555. London, Bibliographical Society, 1944. 111p. 8 plates.

815. _____. English binding before 1500. Cambridge, Univ. Press, 1929. 58p.

816. Jackson, William A. "English title-labels to the end of the 17th century." Harvard library bulletin 2:222-29, spring 1948.

817. Ker, Neil R. Fragments of medieval manuscripts used as pastedowns in Oxford bindings with a survey of Oxford binding c.1515-1620. Oxford, Printed for the Oxford Bibliographical Society by A. T. Broome, 1954. 278p. and plates. (Oxford Bibliographical Society publications n.s. 5)

818. Mitchell, William S. A history of Scottish bookbinding 1432 to 1650. Edinburgh, Oliver and Boyd, 1955. 150p. 48 plates.

    Contains a census of bookbindings of Francis van Hagen, p.129-31.

819. _____. "A history of Scottish bookbinding to 1650, with special reference to the work of Francis van Hagen, bookbinder in Aberdeen." Ph.D. dissertation, Univ. of Aberdeen, 1951.

820. Morris, John. "Thomas Thomas, printer to the University of Cambridge 1583-88. Some account of his materials and bookbindings...." Trans. of the Cambridge Bibliographical Society 4:339-62. 1968.

821. Nixon, Howard M. "Early English gold-tooled bookbindings." (In Studi di bibliografia e di storia: In honore di Tammaro de Marinis. Verona, Valdonega, 1964. vol. 3, p.283-308)

822. _____. "Elizabethan gold-tooled bookbindings." (In Essays in honor of Victor Scholderer. Mainz, Pressler, 1970. p.219-70)

823. _____. "William Caxton and bookbinding." Journal of the Printing Historical Society 11:92-113. 1976/77.

824. Oldham, James B. Blind panels of English binders. Cambridge, Univ. Press, 1958. 55p. 67 plates.

825. _____. English blind-stamp bindings. Cambridge, Univ. Press, 1952. 72p. 61 plates.

826. _____. "English fifteenth century binding." (In Festschrift Ernst Kyriss. Stuttgart, Hettler, 1961. p.159-74)

827. Pollard, Graham. "The construction of English twelfth-century bindings." Library 17:1-22, Mar. 1962.

828. _____. "Some Anglo-Saxon bookbindings." Book collector 24:130-59, spring 1975.

829. Smith, George and Benger, Frank. A collection of armorial book-bindings of the Tudor, Stuart, and Hanoverian period. London, Ellis, 1927. 53p.

17th and 18th Centuries

830. Acland-Troyte, J. E. "An account of the Harmonies contrived by Nicholas Ferrar at Little Gidding." Archeologia 51:189-204. 1888.

831. Almack, Edward. Fine old bindings in Edward Almack's library. London, Blades, East and Blades, 1913. 140p. plates.

      Contains 17th century English bindings.

832. Andrews, William L. Roger Payne and his art. N.Y., Printed at the De Vinne Press, 1892. 35p. plates, facs.

833. Barber, Giles and Rogers, David. "Some seventeenth-century straw bindings." Bodleian library record, June 1971, p.262-65.

834. Chalmers, John P. "Thomas Sedgley, Oxford binder." Book collector 26:353-70, autumn 1977.

835. Craig, Maurice J. "Eighteenth century Irish bookbindings." Burlington magazine 94:132-36, May 1932.

836. _____. "Irish bookbinding." Apollo 84:322-25, Oct. 1966.

837. _____. Irish bookbindings 1600-1800. London, Cassell, 1954. 47p. 58 plates.

838. _____. "Irish parliamentary bindings." Book collector 2:24-38, spring 1953.

839. Davenport, Cyril J. Cameo book-stamps figured and described. London, Edward Arnold, 1911. 207p. illus.

840. _____. "Little Giddings bindings." Bibliographica 2:129-49. 1896.

      Bindings made by an Anglican English community (Little Gidding) in the 17th century.

841. Doyle, A. I. "Hugh Hutchinson, bookbinder of Durham." Book collector 24:25-32, spring 1975.

842. Foxon, David. "Stitched books." Book collector 24:111-24, spring 1975.

843. A general note of the prices of binding all sorts of books; agreed on by the bookbinders, whose names are underwritten. As it was presented to the master, wardens, and assistant of the Worshipful Company of Stationers, August 2, 1669. [London] Broadside 50 by 40cm.

      Reproduced by Harvard University Printing Office in 1951.

844. Hanson, T. W. "Edwards of Halifax: a family of booksellers, collectors and bookbinders." Trans. of the Halifax Antiquarian Society 5:141-200, Nov. 1912.

845. Hobson, Anthony. "Golden age of gilt." Times literary supplement, Aug. 23, 1974, p.910.

   A review of H. M. Nixon's English Restoration bookbindings (1974).

846. Howe, Ellic. The London bookbinders, 1780-1806. London, Dropmore Press, 1950. 182p.

847. Lister, Raymond. "Roger Payne, bookbinder, 1738-97." (In Great craftsmen. London, Bell, 1962. p.133-44)

848. Loudon, J. H. James Scott and William Scott, bookbinders. London, Scolar Press in association with the National Library of Scotland, 1980. 414p. illus.

   Contains descriptions of all known Scott bindings and full-page reproductions of all but a few. See review by Dennis Doughty in Bibliotheck 10, no. 3, p.78-82.

849. Maycock, Alan L. Nicholas Ferrar of Little Gidding. N.Y., Macmillan, 1938. 322p. illus. plates. facs.

   Nicholas Ferrar (1592-1637) was an English deacon who founded an Anglican religious community (Little Gidding). He wrote books which were printed and bound by members of the community.

850. Middleton, Bernard C. "The bookbinder's case unfolded." Library 17:66-76, Mar. 1962.

   About a broadside (printed before 1695) giving detailed description of bookbinding in England.

851. Mitchell, William S. "Aberdeen corner-square bindings." Apollo 53:17-20, Jan. 1951.

852. Nixon, Howard M. "English bookbindings in the Restoration period." Sandars Lectures, Cambridge, 1968. (Typescript in British Library)

853. _____. English Restoration bookbindings: Samuel Mearne and his contemporaries. London, British Museum, 1974. 48p. 126 plates (exhibit catalog)

854. _____. "Harleian bindings." (In Studies in the book trade in honour of Graham Pollard. Oxford, Oxford Bibliographical Society, 1975. p.153-94)

855. _____. "The memorandum book of James Coghlan: the stock of an 18th century printer and binder." Journal of the Printing Historical Society 6:33-52. 1970.

856. _____. "Roger Bartlett's bookbindings." Library 17:56-65, Mar. 1962.

857. Plomer, Henry R. "More petitions to Archbishop Laud: the makers of embroidered bindings." Library 10:129-32, July 1919.

858. Ramsden, Charles. "Richard Wier and Count McCarthy-Reagh." Book collector 2:247-57, winter 1953.

    Richard Wier was a late 18th century English binder. The binding world knew him by the name of David or Davy Wier.

859. Smith, George and Benger, Frank. A collection of armorial bookbinding of the Tudor, Stuart, and Hanoverian period. London, Ellis, 1927. 53p.

860. Sommerlad, Michael J. Scottish 'wheel' and 'herringbone' bindings in the Bodleian Library: an illustrated handlist. Oxford, Oxford Bibliographical Society, 1967. 10p. 3 plates. 27 illus.

861. Sullivan, Edward. "Irish bookbinding; decorative bookbinding in Ireland." Bulletin of the Irish Georgian Society 17, nos. 3/4:3-34. 1974.

862. _____. "Ornamental bookbinding in Ireland in the eighteenth century." International studio 27:52-59, Nov. 1905.

19th Century

863. Adams, John. The House of Kitcat: a story of bookbinding 1798-1948. London, G. & J. Kitcat, 1948. 64p.

864. Allen, Sue. Victorian bookbindings; a pictorial survey. rev. ed. Chicago, Univ. of Chicago Press, 1976. 53p. and 3 microfiche sheets.

    The period is 1825 to the early 1900s. "List of books illustrated," p. 39-53.

865. Andrews, William L. An English 19th century sportsman, bibliopole and binder of angling books. N.Y., 1906. 59, 8p. illus. plates.

    About Thomas Gosden (1780-1840).

866. Barber, Giles. "Rossetti, Ricketts, and some English publishers' bindings of the nineties." Library 25:314-30, Dec. 1970.

867. Calloway, Stephen. Charles Ricketts, subtle and fantastic decorator. London, Thames and Hudson, 1979. 100p. 133 illus.

868. Carter, John. Binding variants in English publishing, 1820-1900. London, Constable, 1932. 172p. 16 collotype plates.

869. _____. More binding variants. London, Constable, 1938. 52p.

870. _____. Publisher's cloth; an outline history of publisher's binding in England 1820-1900. N.Y., Bowker, 1935. 48p.

871. Cave, Roderick. "Cobden-Sanderson: bookbinder." Private library
1:127-36, winter 1968.

872. Cobden-Sanderson, Thomas J. "Bookbinding." (In Arts and crafts
essays by members of the Arts and Crafts Exhibition Society. London,
Rivington, Percival, 1893. p.134-48)

873. _____ . Four lectures. Ed. by John Dreyfus. San Francisco,
Book Club of California, 1974. 105p. illus.

    Contains an essay on Cobden-Sanderson's life and ideals by John
    Dreyfus.

874. _____ . Journals...1879-1922. London, The Author, 1926.
2 vols. illus.

875. Cockerell, Douglas. "Fine bookbinding in England." (In Holme,
Charles, ed. The art of the book. London, Studio, 1914. p.69-121)

876. Colton, Arthur. "Bookbinding in England 1800-1900." Graphic arts
monthly 45:130-32, Sept. 1973.

877. Comparato, Frank E. "England: the book beautiful." (In Books
for the millions. Harrisburg, Pa., Stackpole, 1971. p.41-72)

878. Cook, Davidson. "Illustrations on bindings." Time literary supplement, Apr. 17, 1937, p.296.

879. Darley, Lionel S. Bookbinding then and now; a survey of the first
hundred and seventy-eight years of James Burn and Co. London, Faber
and Faber, 1959. 126p. illus.

880. Darracott, Joseph. The world of Charles Ricketts. London,
Methuen, 1980. 200p. illus.

881. Delaney, Paul. "Book design; a nineteenth-century revival."
Connoisseur 198:283-89, Aug. 1978.

    About Charles Ricketts (1866-1931), English painter, sculptor,
    wood engraver, book designer, and writer on art.

882. _____ . "Father of the well-made book, Charles Ricketts,
designer (1866-1931)." Country life 157:218-19, Jan. 23, 1975.

883. Dibdin, Thomas F. [Charles Lewis] (In Bibliographical decameron...
London, Shakespeare Press, 1817. p.520-23)

884. "English publishers' bindings 1800-1900." New York Public Library
bulletin 40:655-64, Aug. 1936.

885. Farleigh, John. "The arts and crafts exhibition society." Studio
130:137-47, Nov. 1945.

886. Fern, Alan M. "Graphic design." (In Art nouveau. Ed. by Peter
Selz and Mildred Constantine. N.Y., Museum of Modern Art, 1959.
p.18-45)

887. Franklin, Colin. "On the binding of Kelmscott Press books."
Journal of the William Morris Society 2, no. 4:28-30. 1970.

888. Grieve, Alastair. "Rossetti's applied art designs: bookbindings."
Burlington magazine 115:79-84, Feb. 1973.

889. Guild of Women Binders, London. The bindings of tomorrow. A record
of the work of the Guild of Women Binders and of the Hampstead Bindery.
With a critical introduction by G. Elliott Anstruther. London, Williams
and Norgate, 1902. 32p. 50 colored plates.

890. Hammelmann, H. A. "Bookbinder with a noble touch. The Comte de
Caumont." Country life 136:1573-74, Dec. 3, 1964.

    Auguste Marie de Caumont (1743-1833) was a French nobleman who
    conducted a binding workshop in London. Between 1796 and 1814 his
    Soho shop produced elegant bindings.

891. Hobson, Anthony R. "William Beckford's binders." (In Festschrift
Ernst Kyriss. Stuttgart, Hettler, 1961. p.375-82)

    His binders were Christian S. Kalthoeber, Derôme le jeune, Charles
    Smith, Charles Lewis, John MacKenzie, John Wright, and J. Clarke.

892. Howe, Ellic. "London bookbinders; masters and men, 1780-1840."
Library 1:28-38, June 1946.

893. _____ and Child, John. The Society of London Bookbinders,
1780-1951. London, Sylvan Press, 1952. 288p.

894. Jamieson, Eleanore. English embossed bindings 1825-1850.
Cambridge, Univ. Press, 1972. 95p. 59 plates.

895. Jervis, Simon. High Victorian design. Le style de la grande
époque victorienne. A travelling exhibition organized by the Victoria
and Albert Museum for the National Programme of the National Gallery of
Canada, Ottawa. Ottawa, National Gallery of Canada, 1974. 300p. illus.
(In English and French)

    See illustrations of English bindings on p.41-43, 76-78, 107-08,
    136-38, 173-75, 203-06, 231-33 and 265-68.

896. McLean, Ruari. "Styles in nineteenth century publishers' bindings."
(In Victorian book design and colour printing. 2d ed. London, Faber and
Faber, 1972. p.207-26)

897. _____ . Victorian book design and colour printing. 2d ed.
London, Faber and Faber, 1972. 241p. illus.

    Contains many illustrations of bindings, some in color. See bind-
    ings designed by Henry Noel Humphreys, Owen Jones, Robert Dudley,
    Laurence Housman, and Dante G. Rossetti.

898. _____ . Victorian publishers' book-bindings in cloth and leather.
London, Gordon Fraser, 1974. 160p. 16p. of color plates. 128 mono-
chrome plates.

899. Marks, Judith G. "Bookbinding practices of the Hering family 1789-1844." British Library journal 6:44-60, spring 1980.

900. _____. "A study of the bookbinding practices of the Hering family 1794-1844." Master's thesis, Univ. of Chicago, 1969.

901. "Mr. Christopher Dean, designer and illustrator." Studio 12:183-87. 1897/98.

902. "Mr. Charles Lewis." Gentleman's magazine 6:439-40, Oct. 1836.

903. Morris, A. F. "A versatile art worker: Mrs. Traquair." Studio 34:339-43. 1905.

904. Nordhoff, Evelyn H. "The Doves Bindery." Chapbook 4:353-70, Mar. 1, 1896.

905. Nordlunde, C. Volmer. Thomas James Cobden-Sanderson, bogbinder og bogtrykker. Copenhagen, Busck, 1957. 79p. illus. facs.

906. Pantazzi, Sybille. "Four designers of English publishers' bindings, 1850-1880, and their signatures." Publications of the Bibliographical Society of America 55:88-99, 2d quarter 1961.

   The four designers are William Harry Rogers, Albert Henry Warren, Robert Dudley, John Sliegh (or Sleigh).

907. _____. "Versatile Victorian designer: his design for book covers: John Leighton, 1822-1912." Connoisseur 152:262-73, Apr. 1963.

908. Parkes, Kineton. The Sutherland binding, a description and appreciation [with notes on G. T. Bagguley]. Newcastle-under-Lyme, 1900. 15p. illus. (printed for private circulation)

   The Sutherland bindings were made for the Duchess of Sutherland by G. T. Bagguley of Newcastle-under-Lyme. Léon V. Solon was the designer.

909. Pierpont Morgan Library, N.Y. Bookbindings by T. J. Cobden-Sanderson; an exhibition at the Pierpont Morgan Library, Sept.3-Nov. 4, 1968. Comp. by Frederick B. Adams. N.Y., 1969. 32p. 36p. of plates.

910. Prideaux, Sarah T. A catalog of books bound by S. T. Prideaux between 1890-1900, with twenty-six illustrations. London, Printed by S. T. Prideaux and K. Adams, 1900. 20p. 26 plates.

911. _____. "Modern English binding." (In Modern bookbindings, their design and decoration. London, Constable, 1906. p.3-58)

912. _____. "Some Scottish bindings of the last century." Magazine of art 18:110-14, Jan. 1895.

913. Ricketts, Charles S. Charles Ricketts, R. A.; sixty-five illustrations introduced by T. Sturge Moore. London, Cassell, 1933. 19p. 60 plates.

914. Rivière, Robert and Son, London. Examples of bookbinding executed by Robert Rivière and Son exhibited at the Leipzig exhibition in 1914. London, 1920. 36p. 32 plates.

915. _____. Examples of modern bookbinding executed by Robert Rivière and Son. London, Quaritch, 1919. 2p. 69 plates.

916. _____. Photographs of fine bindings. London, 1910? 165 mounted photographs on 39 leaves.

917. Sadleir, Michael. The evolution of publishers' binding styles 1770-1900. London, Constable, 1930. 96p. 12 plates.

918. _____. XIX century fiction; a bibliographical record. London, Constable, 1951. 2 vols. plates.

     Plates of bindings at end of each volume.

919. Schmidt-Künsemüller, Friedrich A. T. J. Cobden-Sanderson as book-binder. Translated [from the German] by I. Grafe. Esher, Tabard Press, 1966. 33p. plates.

920. Spencer, Isabel. Walter Crane. London, Studio Vista, 1975. 208p. illus.

     Appendices A and B supplement G. C. Massé's Bibliography of first editions of books illustrated by Walter Crane (1923).

921. Strange, Edward F. "Decorative work of Gleeson White." Library 1:11-18. 1900.

922. [Sutherland bookbindings] Studio 12:122-24. 1897/98.

     Contains 5 illustrations of bindings. Includes information about G. T. Bagguley and Léon V. Solon.

923. Taylor, John R. [Aubrey Beardsley] (In The art nouveau book in Britain. Edinburgh, Paul Harris, 1979. p.93-103)

924. _____. [Charles Ricketts] (In The art nouveau book in Britain. Edinburgh, Paul Harris, 1979. p.71-92)

925. Weber, Carl J. "Charles Ricketts and his books." Colby library quarterly 4:53-57, Nov. 1951.

926. White, Gleeson. "Artistic decoration of book-covers." Studio 4:15-23, Oct. 1894.

927. Wood, Esther. "British tooled bookbindings and their designers." Studio, special winter no. 1899/1900, p.38-47.

928. _____. "British trade bookbindings and their designers." Studio, special winter no. 1899/1900, p.3-37.

20th Century

929. Abbey, John R. An exhibition of modern English and French bindings
from the collection of Major J. R. Abbey. London, Arts Council, 1949.
30p. plates.

930. Burdett, Eric. "The work of Ivor Robinson." Designer Bookbinders
review 2:9-13. 1973/74.

931. Coldwell, Joan. "'Images that yet fresh images beget': a note on
book covers." (In The world of W. B. Yeats. Ed. by Robin Skelton and
Ann Saddlemyer. rev. ed. Seattle, Univ. of Wash. Press, 1965. p.134-39)

> About the art work of the wood engraver T. Sturge Moore for the
> books of the English poet William Butler Yeats.

932. Designer Bookbinders. Designer Bookbinders 1974. London, Crafts
Advisory Committee, 1974. 72p. illus. (exhibit catalog)

933. _____ . Modern British bookbinders; an exhibition of modern
British bookbinding by members of Designer Bookbinders. London, 1971.
63p. illus.

934. _____ . Two modern binders: William Matthews and Edgar
Mansfield. [catalog of an exhibition] 12 Apr. until 24 June 1978.
London, 1978. 18p. 8 leaves of plates.

935. Duval, K. D., firm, Edinburgh. British bookbinding today. With an
introduction by Edgar Mansfield. Frenich, Foss, Pitlochry, Scotland,
1975. 65p. 39 illus. (many in color)

936. Easton, Malcolm. T. Sturge Moore (1870-1944); contributions to
the art of the book and collaboration with Yeats. Hull, Univ. of Hull,
1970. 55p. illus. (exhibit catalog)

> For a list of books for which he made wood engravings for bindings
> see Frederick L. Gwynn's Sturge Moore and the life of art
> (Lawrence, Univ. of Kansas Press, 1951)

937. Edmiston, Susan. "The bookmaking of Virginia and Leonard Woolf."
Craft horizons 34:24-25, 48-49, Aug. 1974.

> A few years after the Woolfs were married they began the Hogarth
> Press. "For many years we gave much time and care to finding
> beautiful, uncommon, and sometimes cheerful paper for binding our
> books."--Leonard Woolf. Many were bound in marbled paper, such as
> Edwin Muir's Chorus of the newly dead with its splashes of red,
> pumpkin and cream.

938. Elkind, M. Wieder. "Jewelled bindings 1900-1939." Book collector
24:401-16, autumn 1975.

> Francis Sangorski and George Sutcliffe revived the art of jewelled
> leather bindings in London.

939. Gibstone, J. C. "Scots firm are bookbinders to the world."
Scotland's magazine 70:22-24, Aug. 1974.

      About Dunn and Wilson in Falkirk, Scotland.

940. Harrop, Dorothy A. "Anthony Gardner." Book collector 22:169-75,
summer 1973.

941. _____. "Bernard Chester Middleton." Book collector 26:329-41,
autumn 1977.

942. _____. "Charles Philip Smith." Book collector 27:169-90,
summer 1978.

943. _____. "Elizabeth Greenhill." Book collector 28:199-209,
summer 1979.

944. _____. "English bookbinders 1893-1968." M. A. thesis, Univ.
College, London, 1969.

945. _____. "George Fisher and the Gregynog Press." Book collector
19:465-77, winter 1970.

946. _____. "H. J. Desmond Yardley 1905-72." Book collector
24:245-50, summer 1975.

947. _____. A history of the Gregynog Press. Pinner (Middlesex,
England), Private Libraries Association, 1980. 266p. illus. plates.

948. _____. "Jeff Clements." Book collector 25:507-13, winter 1976.

949. _____. "Roger Powell." Book collector 22:479-86, winter 1973.

950. _____. "Sydney Morris Cockerell." Book collector 23:171-78,
summer 1974.

951. Holmes, Kenneth. "Craftsmanship in leather binding: the work of
John Mason and W. J. Westwood." Studio 132:122-23, Oct. 1946.

952. Howe, Ellic and Child, John. The society of London bookbinders
1780-1951. London, Sylvan Press, 1952. 288p.

953. Indiana University. Lilly Library. British bookbinding today.
With an introduction by Edgar Mansfield. Bloomington, 1976. 65p. illus.

954. Mansfield, Edgar. "Bookbinding design; the contemporary approach."
Studio 156:180-83, Dec. 1958.

955. _____. Modern design in bookbinding work. London, Peter Owen,
1966. 119p. 76 full-page plates.

956. Meyer, J. J. de L. "Fine binding as a contemporary art."
Penrose annual 58:237-48. 1965.

957. Nixon, Howard M. Roger Powell and Peter Waters. Froxfield, 1965.
pages? plates. (unverified)

958. Oliver, Cordelia. _Jesse M. King 1875-1949_. Glasgow, Scottish Arts Council, 1971. 58p. illus.

959. Parsons, Ian. "Design in publishers' bindings." _Penrose annual_ 45:48-50. 1951.

960. Pierpont Morgan Library, N.Y. _Modern British bookbinders; an exhibition of modern British bookbinding by members of Designer Bookbinders_ [exhibition Oct. 19-Nov. 1971] N.Y., 1971. 63p. 31 illus.

961. Preston, Emily. "Modern tendencies in bookbinding." _Independent_ 69:1266-71, Dec. 8, 1910.

    Includes England, France, and the United States.

962. "Roger Powell and Peter Waters." _Connoisseur_ 153:244-49, Aug. 1963.

963. S., E. B. "Mr. Talwin Morris's designs for cloth bindings." _Studio_ 15:38-44. 1898/99.

964. Sotheby Parke Bernet and Co. _Jessie M. King and E. A. Taylor: illustrator and designer_. London, 1977. 94p. illus. (auction catalog)

965. Symons, A. J. "Postwar English bookbinding." _Book collector's quarterly_ no. 13:1-6, Jan.-Mar. 1934.

966. Taylor, John R. _The art nouveau book in Britain_. Edinburgh, Paul Harris, 1979. 175p. illus.

    Contains information about Jessie M. King, Talwin Morris, and Laurence Housman. For more book covers designed by Mr. Housman see the National Book League's exhibition catalog on the three Housmans published in 1975.

967. Victoria and Albert Museum, London. "Fine binding." (In _The open and closed book: contemporary book arts, 12 Sept.-18 Nov. 1979_. London, 1979. p.37-48)

968. Watson, Walter R. "Miss Jessie M. King and her work." _Studio_ 26:177-88. 1902.

969. Worsdall, Francis. "Art nouveau and Talwin Morris." _Apollo_ 85:64-65, Jan. 1967.

Hebrew

970. Edelman, R. "Hebraiske boger med solvbind." (In _Fund og forskning i det kongelige bibliotheks samlinger_, vol. 7, p.128-39. 1961)

    On Hebrew silver bindings.

971. Elbogen, Ismar. "Gebetbücher." _Jüdisches Lexikon,_ vol. 2, columns 906-13. 1928.

972. Husung, Max J. "Über den sogenannten jüdischen Lederschnitt."
Soncino-Blätter 1:29-43, Oct. 1925.

Hungary

973. Allen, Walter. "The four Corvinus manuscripts in the United States."
Bulletin of the New York Public Library 42:315-23, Apr. 1938.

974. "The art of the book in Hungary." (In Holme, Charles, ed. The art
of the book. London, Studio, 1914. p.231-42)

975. Belgrade. Museum of Applied Arts. Bindings and metal book plant-
ings from Yugoslav collections. Belgrade, 1973. 80p. illus.
(unverified)

976. Bibliotheca Corviniana; the library of King Matthias Corvinus of
Hungary. Shannon, Ireland, Irish Univ. Press, 1969. 398p. plates.

     Published with the assistance of UNESCO. The volume describes
     manuscripts preserved in libraries outside Hungary and includes
     Ilona Berkovits's Illuminated manuscripts from the library of
     Matthias Corvinus (1964), which describes the manuscripts preserved
     in Hungary.

977. Csapodi, Csaba. The Corvinian library, history and stock. Trans.
by Imre Gombos. Translation revised by László András. Budapest,
Akadémiai Kiadó, 1973. 516p.

     Contains 7 appendices: concordance list, list of places of preser-
     vation, authentic Corvinian codices listed in the present repertor-
     ium, types of coats of arms, list of abbreviations, index of names
     of scribes and illuminators, and index of names of possessors.

978. Fitz, Jozsef. "Mátyás Király, a könyvbarát." (In Mátyás Király
emlékkönyv. Budapest, 1940. vol. 2, p.209-49)

979. Fraknoi, Vilmos. Hunyadi Mátyás Király, 1440-1490. Budapest, 1890.
416p. illus. plates.

     A biography of Matthias I Corvinus, king of Hungary from 1458 to
     1490 and a great book collector. Some of the manuscript volumes
     were bound in leather and velvet and decorated with inlays of vari-
     colored leathers, cameos, and precious stones.

980. Gulyás, Paul. "Entwicklungsgeschichte der Buckbinderei in Ungarn."
Zeitschrift für Bücherfreunde 6:182-97. 1914/15.

981. Halász, Margit. "Batikolt könyvkötések magyarországon." Magyar
könyvszemle 82:138-44, Apr. 1966.

982. Hunyady, József. A magyar könyvkötés müvészete a Mohácsi vészig.
Budapest, Attila-Nyomda, 1937. 111p. illus. plates.

983. Koroknay, Eva S. Ateliers de reliures de la renaissance en Hongrie.
Exposition de reliures hongroises 1470-1520. Budapest, 1966-67. 61p.
illus. 24 plates.

984. _____. "Die Blinddruck Einbände in der Bibliotheca Corvina und
die Probleme der klösterlichen Buchbinderwerkstätten in Ungarn." Acta
historiae artium academiae scientiarum Hungaricae 11 1-2, 95-132. 1965.

985. _____. Magyar reneszánsz könyvkötések; kolostori és polgári
mühelyek. Budapest, Adadémiai Kiadó, 1973. 125p. 64 plates.

     About renaissance monastery and city workshops.

986. Mazal, Otto. "Die Einbände für die Konige Matthias I Corvinus und
Wladislaw II von Hungarn in der Oesterreichischen Nationalbibliothek."
Gutenberg Jahrbuch 1964, p.354-69.

987. Romhányi, Karoly. A magyar könyvkötes müvészete a xviii-xix
szazadban. Budapest, 1937. 340p. plates.

988. Schütz, Géza. "Bibliotheca Corvina." Library quarterly 4:552-63,
Oct. 1934.

989. Schunke, Ilse. "Vom Stil der Corvineneinbände." Gutenberg Jahrbuch
1944/49, p.209-27.

990. Szabó, György. Corvinian manuscripts in the United States, a bibliography. N.Y., Kossuth Foundation, 1960. 20 leaves.

991. Végh, Gyula. Old Hungarian bookbindings. Gyoma, Kner, 1937. 20p.
plates. (In English and German)

992. Victoria and Albert Museum, London. "Illuminated manuscripts and
incunabula." (In Hungarian art treasures. [Exhibition] 11 Oct. 1967-14
Jan. 1968. London, 1968. p.53-66)

     Gives very brief descriptions for manuscripts and printed books
     on display.

India

993. Irwin, John and Hall, Margaret. Indian embroideries. Ahmedabad,
Calico Museum of Textiles, 1973. 222p. plates.

     Contains description for 22 embroidered book covers in the Calico
     Museum of Textiles.

994. Jaina art and architecture. Ed. by A. Ghosh. New Delhi, Bharatiya
Jnanpith, 1975. 3 vols. illus. plates.

     See p.402, plates 266-70A, and colored illustrations 22, 23A-D.

Islam

(See also individual countries)

Reference

995.   Cresswell, K. A.   "Bookbinding."   (In A bibliography of the architecture, arts and crafts of Islam to 1st Jan. 1960.   American Univ. at Cairo Press, 1961.   columns 607-23.   Supplement 1973, columns 199-202)

996.   Gratzl, Emil et al.   "Bibliographie der islamischen Einbandkunst 1871 bis 1956."   Ars orientalis 2:519-40.   1957.

General Works

997.   Abd al-Latif, Ibrahim.   "Jilda mushaf bi-dar al-kutub al-misriya." Bulletin of the Faculty of Arts, Cairo University 20, pt.1:81-107.   1962.

On Koran bindings in the Egyptian National Library.

998.   Adam, Paul.   "Beiträge zur Entwicklung der frühislamischen Einbände."   Archiv für Buchbinderei 14:90-97.   1914.   15:20-30.   1915.

999.   Deleted.

1000.   Aslanapa, Oktay.   "The art of bookbinding."   (In Gray, Basil, ed. The arts of the book in central Asia 14th-16th centuries.   Paris, UNESCO, 1979.   p.59-92)

1001.   Bosch, Gulnar K.   "Islamic bookbindings: twelfth to seventeenth centuries."   Ph.D., Univ. of Chicago, 1952.   238p.

1002.   Chicago.   Art Institute.   A loan exhibition of Islamic bindings, the Oriental Dept., the Art Institute of Chicago, Mar. 20 to May 20, 1932. Chicago, 1932.   31p.   plates.

1003.   Dimand, M. S.   "Bookbinding."   (In Handbook of Muhammadan art. 3d ed.   N.Y., Metropolitan Museum of Art, 1958.   p.79-84)

1004.   Gardner, K. B.   "Oriental bookbindings at the British Museum." Oriental art 9:134-45, Autumn 1963.

1005.   Gratzl, Emil.   Islamische Bucheinbände des 14. bis 19. Jahrhunderts. Leipzig, 1924.   36p.

1006.   Kühnel, Ernst.   "Book bindings."   (In Islamic arts.   London, Bell, 1970.   p.75-81)

1007.   Levey, Martin.   "Medieval Arabic bookmaking and its relation to early chemistry and pharmacology."   Trans. of the American Philosophical Society 52, pt. 4, 1962.

Contains a translation of al Sufyani's work on art of bookbinding and gilding from the Arabic text published by P. Ricard in 1925.

1008. Loubier, Jean. "Orientalische Einbandkunst." Archiv für Buchbinderei 10:33-43, June 1910.

1009. Meyer-Riefstahl, A. M. "La décoration du livre oriental."
Art et décoration 32:33-46. 1912.

1010. Pedersen, Johannes. "Bogbind." (In Den arabiske bog. Copenhagen,
Fischer, 1946. p.100-14)

1011. Petersen, Theodore C. "Early Islamic bookbindings and their
Coptic relations." Ars orientalis 1:41-64. 1954.

1012. Robinson, Basil W. "Book covers and lacquer." (In Islamic painting and the arts of the book. Ed. by B. W. Robinson. London, Faber and
Faber, 1976. p.301-08)

1013. Rodenberg, Julius. Buchkunst des Morgenlandes. Leipzig, 1948.
6p. 25 plates.

1014. Sarre, Friedrich P. Islamic bookbindings. London, Kegan Paul,
Trench, Trübner, 1923. 167p. plates.

       Published also in German in 1923.

1015. Weisweiler, Max. Der islamische Bucheinband des Mittelalters nach
Handschriften aus deutschen, holländischen, und türkischen Bibliotheken.
Wiesbaden, Harrassowitz, 1962. 193p. plates.

                              Italy

Collections of Plates and Illustrations

1016. Abbey, John R. French and Italian collectors and their bindings,
illustrated from examples in the library of John Roland Abbey, by A. R.
A. Hobson. Oxford, Printed for presentation to the members of the
Roxburghe Club, 1953. 190p. illus.

1017. Bologna, Giulia. Museo delle legature Weil Weiss alla Trivulziana.
Milan, Electa, 1976. 243p. 437 illus. facs.

1018. Milan. Archivo Storico Civico. I tesori della trivulziana; la
storia del libro viii al secolo xviii. Commune di Milano, 1962. 250p.
plates.(exhibit catalog)

       See p.55-66 and plates 123-59.

1019. Modena. Bibliotheca Estense. Mostra delle legature artistiche
esistenti a Modena. By Tommaso Gnoli. Modena, 1939. 37p. 40 plates.
(exhibit catalog)

1020. Paris. Exposition du Livre Italien, 1926. Catalogue des manuscrits, livres imprimés, reliures. Bois-Colombes, Imprimerie Moderne
des Beaux Arts, 1926. 160p. plates. facs.

1021. Vatican. Biblioteca Vaticana. Legature papali da Eugenio IV a Paolo VI. Vatican City, 1977. 168p. 211 plates (some in color).

General Works

1022. Fava, Domenico et al. Tesori delle biblioteche d'Italia, Emilia e Romagna. Milan, Hoepli, 1932. 694p. illus. plates. facs.

1023. Toldo, Vittorio de. L'arte italiana della legatura del libro. Milan, 1923. 29p. illus. 37 plates.

1024. _____. L'art italien de la reliure du livre. Milan, Bollega di Poesia, 1924. 31p. 37 plates.

   Published in Italian in 1923 and in English in 1925.

Early History to 1700

1025. Beres, Pierre, booksellers, Paris. Bibliothèque Pillone. Paris, 1957. 155p. mounted illus.

   Catalog of exhibition of Pillone bindings.

1026. Dionigi, Giovanni F. "Legature romane alla mostra di Roma secentesca." Dedalo 3:610-24. 1931.

1027. Donati, Lamberto. "La biblioteca privata di Paoli III." Gutenberg Jahrbuch 1977, p.369-74.

   About Canevari bindings.

1028. _____. "La verita sulle legature cosiddette Canevari." Bibliofilia 78:227-49. 1976.

1029. Duplessis, Georges. Reliure italienne du xv^2 siècle en argent niellé. Paris, 1888. 6p. plates.

1030. Evola, N. D. "L'arte delle rilegatura in Palermo." Academie a biblioteche d'Italia 6:160-66. 1932/33.

1031. Fondazione "Georgio Cini," Venice. Centro di Cultura e Civilta. Istituto di Storia dell'arte. Rilegature veneziane del xv e xvi secolo; catalogo a cura di Tammaro de Marinis. Isola di San Giorgio Maggiore, Venezia, settembre-ottobre 1955. Venice, Pozza, 1955. 45p. 38 plates.

1032. Franch, J. A. "La encuadernación napolitana en la segunda mitad del siglo xv." Revista bibliographica y documental 2:391-407. 1948.

1033. Fumagalli, Giuseppe. L'arte della legatura alla corte degli Estensi, a Ferrara e a Modena dal sec. xv al xix. Florence, De Marinis, 1913. 104p. 38 plates.

1034. Hobson, Anthony R. Apollo and Pegasus: an enquiry into the
formation and dispersal of a renaissance library. Amsterdam, Philo
Press-Van Heusden, 1975. 250p. illus. 24 plates.

> A group of 16th century bindings with plaquettes of Apollo and
> Pegasus were thought to belong to a Genoese doctor, Demetrio
> Canevari, until Geoffrey Hobson suggested another owner in his
> 1926 volume, Maioli, Canevari and others (see below). His son,
> Anthony Hobson, in this latest study presents a more convincing
> body of information for a Giovanni Grimaldi, a Genoese nobleman
> and collector (c.1524-1610 or 11 or 12). He identifies the three
> Roman binders: Maestro Luigi, Niccolò Franzese, and Marcontonio
> Guillery. The volume contains a list of Apollo and Pegasus bind-
> ings (p.129-92) and their present and past owners (p.225-28).
> See the following reviews: Book collector 25:563, winter 1976;
> Library quarterly 47:378-79, July 1977; Times literary supplement,
> May 28, 1976, p.654 (by Howard Nixon).

1035. _____. "The Pillone library." Book collector 7:28-37, spring
1958.

> The library was collected by two generations of the Pillone family
> in the 16th century: Antonio and his son Odorico. The binding
> was done in Belluno (Italy), somewhere in the Veneto, and Germany.
> All the volumes are still in their original bindings. The collec-
> tion is famous for the fore-edge paintings by Cesare Vecellio, a
> relative and pupil of Titian.

1036. Hobson, Geoffrey D. Maioli, Canevari and others. London, Benn,
1926. 178p. 64 plates.

> Contains information about two sixteenth century book collectors,
> Thomas Mahieu (Maiolus) and Jean Grolier, and the supposed owner
> of the Canevari bindings. The author suggests that the more prob-
> able owner was not Dr. Demetrio Canevari (1559-1625) but instead
> Pier Luigi Farnese (1503-1574), the son of Alessandro Farnese,
> subsequently Pope Paul III. See note for Anthony Hobson's Apollo
> and Pegasus (1975).

1037. Jodi, Camilla. "L'arte della rilegatura a Modena: Dante Gozzi."
Bibliofilia 29:267-74, Oct./Nov. 1927.

> Contains illustrations of bindings by Dante and Rolando Gozzi.

1038. Juntke, Fritz. "Venezianische Einbände des xvi Jahrhunderts."
Gutenberg Jahrbuch 1957, p. 324-32.

1039. Lanckorońska, Maria. "Der grosse Canevari-mythos." Gutenberg
Jahrbuch 44:300-07. 1969.

1040. Marinis, Tammaro de. Die italienischen Renaissance-Einbände der
Bibliothek Fürstenberg. Hamburg, Maximilian-Gesellschaft, 1966. 190p.
illus.

1041. Marinis, Tammaro de. La bibliotheca napolitana dei re d'Aragona.
Milan, 1947-52. 4 vols. plates. facs. suppl., 1969. 2 vols.

Alfonso V the Magnificent, King of Aragon (Spain), conquered
Naples in 1442 and moved his court there the next year. For his
library he had manuscripts copied, illuminated, and bound.
Skilled leather workers from Granada and Cordoba were imported
to do the binding. During Alfonso's reign the court became a
brilliant center of art and culture. The library was dispersed
toward the end of the century.

1042. _____. La legatura artistica in Italia nei secoli xv e xvi;
notizie ed elenchi. Florence, Fratelli Alinari, Istituto di Edizioni
Artistiche, 1960. 3 vols.

1043. Mazzatinti, Giuseppe. La biblioteca dei re d'Aragona in Napoli.
Rocca S. Casciano, L. Capelli, 1897. 200p.

1044. Paris. Bibliothèque Nationale. Trésors des bibliothèques d'
Italie iv-xvi siècles. 2d ed. Paris, 1950. pages not numbered.
plates.

See entries 336-96 for bindings described for Italian works.

1045. Piquard, M. "Les livres du Cardinal de Granvelle à la bibliothèque
de Besançon: les relieurs italiennes." Libri 1:301-23. 1951.

Antoine Perrenot de Granvelle (1517-1586) was a Spanish cardinal
and statesman. During his residency in Naples (1565-1579) he
built up a fine collection of books and used his leisure for
literary and scientific studies. In 1584 he was named archbishop
of Besançon, France, his native town.

1046. Prideaux, Sarah T. "Early Italian bindings." (In Bookbinders and
their craft. London, Zaehnsdorf, 1903. p.211-66)

1047. Rossi, Filippo. "Le legature italiane del '500." Dedalo
3:373-96, Nov. 1922.

1048. Ryder, Alan F. The Kingdom of Naples under Alfonso the Magnani-
mous: the making of a modern state. Oxford, Clarendon Press, 1976.
409p. illus.

About Alfonso V (1396-1458), King of Aragon and Naples. In the
course of his reign in Naples the library became one of the most
famous in Europe.

1049. Sander, Max. Copertine italiane illustrate del Rinascimento.
Milan, Hoepli, 1936. 19p. 20 plates.

1050. Schunke, Ilse. "Die Entwicklung der Päpstlichen Einbände vom 16.
zum 17. Jahrhundert." (In Collectanea Vaticana in honorem Anselmi M.
Card. Albareda a Biblioteca Apostolica. Vatican, Biblioteca Apostolica
Vaticana, 1962. vol. 2, p.331-54)

1051. Schunke, Ilse. "Der Renaissanceeinbandkunst in Bologna." (In
Beiträge zur Geschichte des Buches und seiner Funktion in der Gesell-
schaft. Festschrift für Hans Widmann zum 65. Ed. by Alfred Swierk.
Stuttgart, Hiersemann, 1974. p.252-68)

1052. _____. "Über die aragonesischen Buchbinder in Neapel."
Gutenberg Jahrbuch 1957, p.315-23.

1053. _____. "Venezianische Einbandkunde." (In Marinis, Tammaro de.
Studi di bibliografia e di storia in onore de Tammaro de Marinis.
Verona, 1964. vol. 4, p.123-200)

1054. _____. "Die vier Meister der Farnese-Platteneinbände."
Bibliofilia 54:57-91. 1952.

       About the famous Canevari bindings. See note for Anthony
       Hobson's Apollo and Pegasus (1975).

1055. Tordi, Domenico. "Ser Agnolo Ferrini, legatore d'incunaboli
(1473-1488)." Bibliofilia 11:182-90. 1909.

1056. Valentinelli, Giuseppe. Di alcune legature antiche di codici
manoscritti liturgici della Marciana di Venezia. Venice, 1867. 18p.
2 plates.

18th through the 20th Century

1057. Jodi, Camilla. "Der moderne künstlerisches Bucheinband in
italien." Jahrbuch der Einbandkunst 2:180-86. 1928.

1058. McLeod, Addison. "Some recent Italian bookbinding." Art journal
59:344-47, Nov. 1907.

1059. Morazzoni, Giuseppe. La rilegature piemontese nel 1700. Milan,
Toscanini, 1929. 69p. 60 plates.

1060. Orzi Smeriglio, Panfilia. Il libro romano del settecento.
La stampa e la legatura. Rome, Tip. dell'Accademia Nazionale dei Lincei,
1959. 134p. 47 plates (exhibit catalog)

1061. Petrucci, Armando. "Sulla legatoria romana dei xviii secolo."
Bibliofilia 63:165-95. 1961.

1062. Santagostino-Sandri, Mario. La legature d'arte. Legni originale
di Italo Zetti. Milan, 1940. 134p. 10 plates.

1063. Vico, Arnaldo dei. L'arte nella legatura moderna, i legatore e
il libro. Rome, 1931. 109p. 24 plates.

Japan

1064. Chibbett, David. "The printed book: binding techniques." (In
The history of Japanese printing and book illustration. Tokyo, Kodansha
International, 1977. p.26-28)

1065. Chibbett, David. "Publishing in the Edo period: engraving, printing, and binding." (In The history of Japanese printing and book illustration. Tokyo, Kodansha International, 1977. p.89-92)

1066. Graham, Rigby. "Early Japanese bookbinding." Private library 6:26-31, April 1965.

1067. Nakatsuchi, Y. "Japan." Dolphin 2:318-29. 1935.

1068. Tokyo, Keizaikyoku. Sōmobu. Chōsaka. Seihongyō no kuttai bunseki. 1965. 74p.

Mexico

1069. Fernandez de Cordoba, Joaquin. Encuadernaciones artisticas de Michoacán. Editorial Arana, 1970. 20p. illus.

1070. Romero de Terreros, Manuel. "Bookbinding in Mexico." Mexican art and life no. 7:34-36, July 1939.

1071. _____. Encuadernaciones artisticas mexicanas siglos xvi al xix. Mexico DF, 1932. 25p. 48 plates. 2d ed., 1943.

Netherlands

(Includes Flanders)

General Works

1072. Oyen, Anthonie A. Vosterman van. Les marques d'imprimeurs. Arnhem, 1910. 12p.

   Contains Dutch printers and binders marks.

1073. Verwey, Herman de la Fontaine. "Amsterdam publishers' bindings from about 1600." Quaerendo 5:283-302. 1975.

Early History to 1700

1074. Bendikson, L. The House of Magnus at Amsterdam, famous book-binders of the 17th century. Los Angeles, 1936. illus.

   Appeared originally in Pacific bindery talk.

1075. Brassinne, Joseph. La reliure mosane. Liège, Cormaux, 1912. 44p. 78 plates.

1076. Colin, Georges and Nixon, Howard M. "La question des reliures de Plantin." (In Studia bibliographica in honorem Herman de la Fontaine Verwey. Amsterdam, Hertzberger, 1968. p.56-89)

1077. Godenne, Willy. Les reliures de Plantin. Brussels, The Author,
1965. 26p. plates.

1078. Horodisch, Abraham. "Hollandische gestickte Einbände." (In
Festschrift Ernst Kyriss. Stuttgart, Hettler, 1961. p.383-96)

1079. Hulshof, Abraham and Schretlen, M. J. De kunst der oude boek-
binders xv ^{de} en xvi ^{de} eeuwsche boekbinder in de Utrechtsche Universiteits-
Bibliotheek. Utrecht, 1921. 59p. plates.

1080. Indestege, Luc. De boekband in de oude Nederlanden. Utrecht,
1951. 23p. illus.

1081. _____. "De boekband in de Zuidelijke Nederlanden tijdens de
16de eeuw." Gulden passer 34:40-71. 1956.

1082. _____. "Einbandkunst in den alten Niederländen. Frühe
flamische Plattenstempel." Gutenberg Jahrbuch 1955, p.239-48.

1083. _____. "Heads-in-medallion panels as binding decoration in
the Netherlands during the sixteenth dentury." (In Studia bibliographica
in honorem Herman de la Fontaine Verwey. Amsterdam, Hertzberger, 1967.
p.276-96)

1084. Schunke, Ilse. "Plantin und die niederländische Einbandkunst
seiner Zeit." Gulden passer 37:122-41. 1959.

1085. Vaernewyck, Amaury G. "La reliure flamande au xv ^{e} siècle." (In
Académie d'archéologie de Belgique. Annales 55:389-416. 1901.

1086. Verheyden, Prosper. "Noord-Nederlandse boekbanden." Het boek
31:197-239. 1952/54.

1087. Verwey, Herman de la Fontaine. "The binder Magnus and the collectors of his age." Quaerendo 1:158-78. 1971.

1088. Wijnman, H. F. "De Amsterdamsche boekbinder Albert Magnus."
Oud-Holland 54:183-92, 230-40. 1937.

18th through the 20th Century

1089. Faasen, Loes. "P.A.H. Hofman (1885-1965), boekbandantwerper en
boekversierder." Open 7:520-33. 1975.

1090. Foot, Mirjam M. "Some Dutch bindings of the seventeenth and early
eighteenth centuries." (In The Henry David gift. A collection of bindings. London, British Library, 1978. vol. 1, p.242-60)

1091. Leeuwen, Jan S. van. "Herleving van de boekbindkunst in
Nederland." Open 7:203-05, Apr. 1975.

1092. Linden, Fons van der. "The rise of cloth in bookbinding and its
introduction to the Netherlands." Quaerendo 6:272-98. 1976.

1093. Mourey, Gabriel. "Dutch bookbindings." Studio, special winter no. 1899-1900, p.66-68.

1094. Stokkink, J. Vijftig jaren boekbinderij in Nederland. Amsterdam, 1950. 30p. illus.

Norway

1095. Bakken, Hilmar. Gerhard Munthes dekorative kunst. Oslo, Gyldendal, 1946. 346p. illus. facs.

1096. Haugstol, Henrik. Med og uten gullsnitt; Oslo bokbindermestres forening 1890-1950. Oslo, Oslo Bokbindermestres Forening, 1950. 203p. illus. facs.

1097. Nygard-Nilssen, Arne. Forlagsbind; en historisk oversikt og litt til. Oslo, 1937. 104p. illus.

1098. Oslo. Kunstindustrimuseet. Gamle bokbind i Norge. Oslo, Moestue, 1925. 73p. illus.

1099. _____. Nye norske bokbind. Oslo, 1933. 40p. illus. (exhibit catalog)

1100. Schjoldager, Astrid. Bokbind og bokbindere i Norge inntil 1850. Oslo, 1927. 348p. illus.

Persia

1101. Aga-Oglu, Mehmet. Persian bookbindings of the fifteenth century. Ann Arbor, Univ. of Michigan Press, 1935. 23p. illus. plates.

1102. Bunt, Cyril G. "Bookbindings in the Victoria and Albert Museum, 3:select Persian bookcovers." Apollo 17:72-79. 1933.

1103. Christensen, Arthur. "Bokhaandvaerk og boghunst i Persien." Aarbog for bogvenner 2:22-46. 1918.

1104. Eisen, Gustavus A. "Arabic and Persian bindings." International studio 80:220-30, Dec. 1924.

1105. Ettinghausen, Richard. "The covers of the Morgan Manâfi manuscript and other Persian bookbindings." (In Studies in art and literature for Belle da Costa Greene. Ed. by Dorothy Miner. Princeton, Princeton Univ. Press, 1954. p.459-73)

1106. Gratzl, Emil. "Book covers." (In Pope, Arthur, ed. Survey of Persian art. London, Oxford Univ. Press, 1939. vol. 3, p.1975-1994)

1107. James, Philip B. "Persian lacquered bookbindings." Studio 96:118-21. 1928.

1108. Sakisian, Arménag. La reliure dans la Perse occidentale, sous les Mongols, au xivᵉ et au début du xvᵉ siècle." Ars islamica 1:80-91. 1934.

1109. _____. "La reliure persane au xvᵉ siècle sous les Timourides." Revue de l'art 66:145-68. 1934.

1110. _____. "La reliure persane au xvᵉ siècle sous les Turcomans." Artibus Asiae 6:210-23. 1937.

Poland

1111. Bochnak, Adam and Buczkowski, Kazimierz. Rzemiosto artystyczne w Polsce. Warsaw, Wydawnictwo Arkady, 1971. 503p. illus. plates.

1112. Gasiorowska, Maria J. and Wierzbicki, M. Oprawy artystyczne xiii-xviii w. Cracow, 1952. 10p. (chiefly illus.)

1113. Halaciński, Kazimierz. O krakowskich introligatorach ubieglego wieku. Cracow, 1926. 27p. plates.

1114. Kafel, Mieczyslaw. Zarys techniki wydawniczej. Warsaw, 1955. 419p. 327 illus.

1115. Lewicka-Kaminska, Anna. "Die Entwicklung der Einbandkunst in Krakow." Zeitschrift für Bibliothekswesen 86:641-58. 1972.

1116. _____. "Rzut oka na rozwoj oprawy ksiazkowej w Krakowie." Roczniki biblioteczne 16: nos. 1-2:49-68. 1972.

1117. Schonath, Wilhelm. "Polnische Einbände in der Graf von Schön-bornschen Schossbibliothek Pommersfelden." Gutenberg Jahrbuch 1962, p.507-11.

1118. Schunke, Ilse. "Krakauer Frührenaissanceeinbände." Gutenberg Jahrbuch 1973, p.429-35.

1119. Warchalowski, Georg. "Die moderne polnische Buchbindekunst." Jahrbuch der Einbandkunst 2:193-201. 1928.

Portugal

1120. Castro e Solla, Amadau. Super-libros ornamentaes. Lisbon, 1913-15. 149p. illus.

1121. Lima, Matias. ...A encadernação em Portugal. Gaia, Edições Patria, 1933. 76p. illus. 45 plates.

1122. _____. Encadernadores portugueses; notulas biographicas e criticas. Porto, 1956. 216p. illus.

1123. _____. Super-libros Portuguezes ineditos. Porto, Machado, 1927. 145p. illus.

Rumania

1124. Bacâru, Livia. "Vechi legături de cărti româneşti." Studii si
cercetari de bibliologie. Serie nouă 13:39-90. 1974.

1125. Musée d'Ethnographie de Neuchâtel. "Ouvrages manuscrits et
imprimés, reliures en argent doré." (In Roumanie trésors des arts.
[Exhibition] 7 juillet 1968 au 5 janvier 1969. Neuchâtel, 1968. p.72-73)

Russia

1126. Beatty, Alfred C. The Chester Beatty Library. A catalogue of
the Armenian manuscripts. Dublin, Hodges Figgis, 1958. 2 vols. facs.

    Contains brief descriptions of bindings and 8 illustrations.

1127. Compton, Susan P. "Graphic design." (In The world backwards:
Russian futurist books 1912-16. London, British Library, 1978. p.67-86)

1128. Ettinger, Paul. "Book wrappers in Soviet Russia." Studio
93:34-37. 1927.

1129. Der Nersessian, Sirarpie. Armenian manuscripts in the Freer
Gallery of Art. Wash., D.C., Freer Gallery of Art, 1963. 131p. 108
plates.

    Contains information on bindings and 2 plates.

1130. Helwig, Hellmuth. "Das Buchbinderhandwerk in Riga vom 16. bis 18.
Jahrhundert." Archiv für Geschichte des Buchwesens 8:columns 485-504.
1967.

1131. Klepikov, S. A. "Historical notes on Ukrainian bookbinding."
Book collector 15:135-42, summer 1966.

1132. _____. "Iz istorii russkogo chodozestvennogo." Kniga.
Issledovanija materialy 1:98-166. 1959.

    A study of Russian binding from the 12th to the 20th century,
    with special attention to early binding.

1133. _____. "Russian bookbinding from the eleventh to the middle
of the seventeenth century." Book collector 10:408-22, winter 1961.

1134. _____. "Russian bookbinding from the middle of the seventeenth
to the end of the nineteenth century." Book collector 11:437-47, winter
1962.

1135. Pokrovskii, N. N. "Western Siberian scriptoria and binderies;
ancient traditions among old believers." Book collector 20:19-24. 1971.

    Appeared in a fuller form in Trudy otdela drevnerusskoi literatury
    24:394-403. 1969.

Spain

Reference

1136. Castañeda y Alcover, Vicente. Ensayo de un diccionario biographico de encuadernadores españoles. Madrid, 1958. 330p.

General Works

1137. Ainaud, Juan. "Encuadernación." Ars Hispaniae 18:323-44. 1962.

1138. Antolin Pajares, G. "Notas acerca de la encuadernación artistica del libro en Espagna." Boletin de la Real Academia de la historia 89:294-308. 1926.

1139. _____. "La encuadernación del libro en España." La Ciudad de Dios. El Escorial 128:422-49. 1922.

1140. Castañeda y Alcover, Vicente. "Notas para la historia del arte de la encuadernación." Boletin de la Real Academia de la historia 142:79-142. 1958.

1141. Goldschmidt, Werner. "Spanish bookbindings from the xiiith to the xixth century." Apollo 20:329-32, Dec. 1934.

1142. Hueso Rolland, Francisco. "Encuadernaciones españolas." Revista española de arte 2:437-44. 1933.

1143. López Serrano, Matilde. Biblioteca de Palacio: encuadernaciones. Madrid, Aguado, 1950. 181p. 79 plates.

1144. _____. La encuadernación española; breve historia. Madrid, Asociación de Bibliotecarios, Archivos y Arquelogos, 1972. 146p. plates.

1145. Madrid. Real Academia de Medicine. La primera fiesta del libro español. Discursos leídos por...Antonio Espina y Capo...y Francisco Xavier Cortezo y Collantes.... Madrid, 1927. 178p. illus.

   The essay by Cortezo y Collantes has the title: "Algo sobre la encuadernación como oficio y como arte en España."

1146. Passola, José M. Artesiania de la piel: encuadernaciones en Vich. Vich, Colomer Munmany, 1968-69. 2 vols. illus.

1147. Penney, Clara L. Album of selected bookbindings. N.Y., Hispanic Society of America, 1967. 18p. 60 plates.

1148. Saltillo, Marqués del. "Encuadernaciones heráldicas españolas." Revista española de arte no. 1:2-35. 1934.

1149. Sociedad Española de Amigos del Arte, Madrid. Exposicion de encuadernaciones españolas, siglos xii al xix; catalogo general ilustrado por Francisco Hueso Rolland. Madrid, 1934. 258p. 61 plates.

Early History to 1700

1150. Castañeda y Alcover, Vicente. <u>Antecedentes y notas sobre la encuadernación valenciana</u>. Madrid, Editorial Maestre, 1949. 43p. illus.

1151. Hueso Rolland, Francisco. "La exposición de encuadernaciones antiguas españolas." <u>Revista española de arte</u> 3:55-65. 1934.

1152. _____. "Encuadernaciones mudéjares." (In Sociedad Español de Amigos del Arte. <u>Exposición de encuadernaciones españoles, siglos xii al xix</u>. Madrid, 1934. p.31-38)

1153. Miguel y Planas, Ramón. <u>Restauración del arte Hispano-Arabe en la decoration exterior de los libros</u>. Barcelona, 1913. 23p. illus. plates.

1154. Salvador, V. F. "Encuadernadores valencianos de los siglos 17 y 18." <u>Revista bibliográfica y documental</u> 2:289-94. 1948.

1155. Thomas, Henry. "Diego Hurtado de Mendoza and his plaquette bindings." (In <u>Studies in art and literature for Belle de Costa Greene</u>. Ed. by Dorothy Miner. Princeton, Princeton Univ. Press, 1954. p.474-80)

1156. _____. <u>Early Spanish bookbindings xi-xv centuries</u>. London, Printed for the Bibliographical Society at the Univ. Press, Oxford, 1939 (for 1936). 65p. plates.

18th and 19th Centuries

1157. López Serrano, Matilde. "La encuadernación madrileña durante el reinado de Carlos III." <u>Archivo español de arte</u> 18:1-17. 1945.

>About Gabriel Gomez (1741?-1818), Gabriel de Sancha (1746-1820), Santiago Martin (1775-1828), and Pascual Carsi y Vidal (fl. 1797-1808).

1158. _____. "La encuadernación madrilena en la época de Carlos IV." <u>Archivo español de arte</u> 23:115-31. 1950.

>Shows bindings of 26 books, including Gabriel de Sancha, José Ramon Herrera, Felix Ximenez, Tomas Novoa, Pascual Carsi y Vidal, Santiago Martin, and Santiago Thevin.

1159. _____. "La encuadernación madrilena en la época de Fernando VI." <u>Archivo español de arte</u> 14:27-38. 1940.

1160. _____. "Encuadernaciones romanicas de España." <u>Bibliographica hispanica</u> 2:2, 8-18. 1943.

1161. _____. "El encuadernador Gabriel Gómez Martín." <u>Revista de bibliographia nacional</u> 6:51-72. 1945.

1162. _____. "Libreros encuadernadores de Cámara: Antonio Suarez." <u>Arte español</u> 14, no. 2:7-14. 1942.

1163. López Serrano, Matilde. "Libreros encuadernadores de Cámara: Santiago Martín." Arte español 14, no. 4:14-22. 1943.

1164. Salvador, V. F. "Encuadernadores valencianos de los siglos 17 y 18." Revista bibliográfica y documental 2:289-94. 1948.

1165. Vindel Alvarez, Pedro. D. Antonio de Sancha, encuadernador. Madrid, 1935. 13p. 27 plates.

20th Century

1166. Armand, Jeanne. "Moderne Einbandkunst in Spanien." Jahrbuch der Einbandkunst 1929/30, p.132-33.

1167. Brugalla, Emilio. "Bookbinders search for new design." Craft horizons 14:28-31, Sept. 1954.

      Contains 10 illustrations of bindings by the author and his son Santiago.

1168. Brugalla: 254 reproducciones de sus destacadas encuadernaciones. Bilbao, La Gran Enciclopedia Vasca, 1977. 559p. illus. (some in color)

1169. López Serrano, Matilde. "Notas caracteristicas de la encuadernatión moderna." Revista bibliográfica y documental 1:7-15. 1947.

1170. Lujan-Muñoz, Jorge. "The beauty of bookbinding." Américas 32: 22-25, May 1980.

      About the work of the José Galván bindery in Cadiz, Spain.

1171. Meyer, J. J. de L. "Fine binding as a contemporary art." Penrose annual 58:237-48. 1965.

Sweden

Reference

1172. Lindberg, Sten G. "Bokbandslitteratur." Biblis 1975, p.188-232.

1173. Rehnberg, Mats E., ed. Bokbinderminnen. Stockholm, Nordiska Museet, 1954. 166p.

Early History to 1800

1174. Collijn, Isak. "Alte schwedische Bucheinbände." Zeitschrift für Bücherfreunde 3:309-26. 1911/12.

1175. Hedberg, Arvid. Bokbindare bokfoerare i Sverige 1500-1630. Stockholm, 1914. 113-254p.

1176. _____. Stockholms bokbindare 1460-1880. Stockholm, 1949-60. 2 vols. illus.

1177. Karlson, William. Bokband och bokbindare i Lund. Lund, 1939.
297p. illus. plates.

1178. Lindberg, Sten G. Bokband i Stockholm under 325 ar. Stockholm,
1959. 26p. illus.

1179. _____. "Bookbindings in Sweden." (In Festschrift Ernst Kyriss.
Stuttgart, Hettler, 1961. p.447-63)

    Includes illustrations of bindings by Kristoffer Schneidler,
    Diedrich Volcker (c.1700), Johan K. Coloander (c.1796) and
    Gustaf Hedberg (c.1905).

1180. _____. "Den svenska bokbandskonstens glansperiod." Biblis
1957. p.71-85.

1181. Rudbeck, Gustaf. Broderade bokband fraan aeldre tid i svenska
samlinger. Stockholm, 1925. 110p. 39 plates.

1182. _____. Schwedische Bucheinbände in der neuren Zeit. Teil 1
(1521-1718). Stockholm, 1910. 156p. illus.

1183. _____. Kristoffer Schneidler. En Stockholms-bokbindare for
150 ar sedan. Stockholm, 1910. 15p. illus.

1184. _____. Svenska bokband under nyare tiden bidrag till svensk
bokbinderhistoria. Stockholm, 1912-14. 3 vols. in 2. illus.

1185. Sjögren, Arthur. Svenska kungliga och furstliga bokagaremarken.
Stockholm, 1915. 354p. illus. plates.

    About Swedish royal bindings.

1186. Wahlstrom, Lars. Bokbinderiboken. Stockholm, Almqvist & Wiksell,
1967. 60p. illus.

18th through the 20th Centuries

1187. Åkerstrom, Sture. "Gust Hedberg hovbokbinderi i Kungl. biblioteket."
Biblis, årsbok, 1971, p.97-138.

1188. Brunius, August. "The art of the book in Sweden." (In Holme,
Charles, ed. The art of the book. London, Studio, 1914. p.243-58)

1189. Ellsworth, Charles. "Hand bookbinding in Sweden." Craft horizons
13:13-15, Jan.-Feb. 1953.

    Contains illustrations of bindings designed by Nils Linde, Nils
    Wedel, William Barkell, Axel Virin, Anders Billow, and Eva Billow.

1190. Frykholm, Sunny. "Bookbinding in Sweden." Studio, special
winter no. 1899/1900, p.78-82.

1191. Hald, Arthur and Skawonius, Sven. Contemporary Swedish design.
Stockholm, Nordisk Rotogravyr, 1951. 179p. illus.

    Contains illustrations of bindings, p.35-37, by Sven Skawonius,
    Per Hedlung, Nils Wedel, Nils Mörck, William Barkell, Hakan
    Wahlström, Carl-Axel Virin, Charles Sjöblom, and Bertil Kumlien.
    List of binderies on p.174-75.

1192. Lindberg, Sten G. "Gustav Hedberg." Biblis 1963/64, p.191-261.

1193. Silfverstolpe, Gunnar M. Bokbindare i Stockholm 1630-1930.
Stockholm, Norstedt, 1930. 242p. plates.

1194. Stockholm. National Museum. Moderna svensk bokband. Stockholm,
Pettersons, 1950. 62p. plates (exhibit catalog).

1195. Wiberg, Carl G. Sveriges bokbinderidkareforening, 75 ar.
Stockholm, Sveriges Bokbinderidkareforening, 1975. 165p. illus.

Switzerland

1196. Baumann, Walter. "Ein Pionier der modernen Buchkunst: Josef
Stemmle zum sechzigsten Geburtstag." Librarium 23:139-49, Sept. 1980.

    Josef Stemmle, a Swiss binder, established the Legatoria Artistica
    in 1965 in Ascona, Switzerland for restoring and rebinding precious
    books. The next year the Galleria del Bel Libro opened as a
    permanent place for exhibiting work by binders from Switzerland,
    France, Germany, Britain, Greece, Spain, Denmark, and Belgium.
    He is now Director of the Centro del Bel Libro in Ascona, a work-
    shop for handmade paper and bindings.

1197. Baur, Albert. "Emil Kretz." Buch und Schrift 10:174-76. 1937.

1198. Bitterli, Rudolf. Das schweizerische Buchbindergewerbe. Zurich,
Polygraphischer Verlag, 1962. 147p. diagrams. tables.

1199. Lindt, Johann. "Berner Buchbinder des 17. und 18. Jahrhunderts."
Berner Zeitschrift für Geschichte und Heimatkunde 35:89-128. 1973.

1200. _____. Berner Einbände, Buchbinder und Buchdrucker. Bern,
Schweizerisches Gutenbergmuseum, 1969. 214p. illus. facs.

1201. _____. "Der Dominikanermonch Johannes Vatter, Buchbinder der
Predigerklosters in Bern." Schweizerisches Gutenbergmuseum 51:9-16.
1965.

1202. _____. "Die Buchbinder Apiarius in Bern und ihre Nachfolger."
Schweizerisches Gutenbergmuseum 51:61-91. 1965.

1203. _____. "Hans Leman, ein Berner Buchbinder." Schweizerisches
Gutenbergmuseum 50:79-89. 1964.

1204. Lonchamp, Frédéric. Manuel du bibliophile suisse. Paris,
Librairie des Bibliophiles, 1922. 440p. illus. plates.

1205. Londenberg, Kurt. "Ascona, ein Zentrum des schönen Buches?"
Philobiblon 13, no. 1:31-42, Jan. 1969.

1206. Mason, Stanley. "Centro del bel libro, Ascona." Graphis no. 196:
114-19. 1978.

     The Centro del bel libro in Ascona is a workshop for handmade
     paper and bindings.

1207. Munby, Alan N. "Windham and Gauffecourt." Trans. of the Cambridge
Bibliographical Society 1:186-90. 1949/53.

     Intermittently between 1738 and 1742 William Windham (1717-61)
     lived in Geneva, where he became interested in binding. Jean-
     Vincent Capronnier Gauffecourt (1692-1766) lived in both Geneva
     and Lyon and is the author of Traité de la reliure (La Motte, 1763),
     the first printed work in French devoted to bookbinding.

1208. Rijksmuseum Meermanno-Westreenianum, The Hague.   Bokbanden uit
het Centro del bel libro, Ascona. [Exhibition] Feb. 7-Apr. 1975. The
Hague, 1975. 36p. 10 illus.

                              Turkey

1209. Arseven, Celal E. "La reliure." (In Les arts décoratifs turcs.
Istanbul, Basimevi, 1952. p.309-20)

1210. Atil, Esin. "The art of the book." (In Turkish art. Ed. by
Esin Atil. Smithsonian Institution and Harry N. Abrams, 1980. p.137-238)

1211. Binark, İsmat. "Türk kitapçilik tarihinde cilt san'ati."
Türk kültürü 3, no. 36:985-96. 1965.

1212. Çiğ, Kemal. "Reliures de livres turcs aux xv-xviii⁰ siècles."
Türkiye no. 1:66-69. 1954.

1213. _____. Türk kitap kaplari. Istanbul, 1971. 72p. illus.
46 plates.

1214. Meriç. Rifki M. Türk cild san'ati tarihi arastirmalari. Ankara,
1954- facs.

1215. Sakisian, Arménag. "La reliure turque du xv⁰ au xix⁰ siècle."
Revue de l'art 51:277-84, May 1927; 52:141-54, 286-98, Sept.-Oct. 1927.

United States

General Works

1216. Andrews, William L. Bibliopegy in the United States and kindred subjects. N.Y., Dodd, Mead, 1902. 128p. 30 illus.

1217. Lehmann-Haupt, Hellmuth et al. Bookbinding in America: three essays. N.Y., Bowker, 1967. 293p.

1218. Poor, Henry W. American bookbindings in the library of Henry William Poor. Described by Henry Pène du Bois. N.Y., G. D. Smith, 1903. 7,p. 39 colored plates.

1219. Thompson, Lawrence S. "Bookbinding in the Americas." Inter-American review of bibliography 7, no. 3, July-Sept. 1962. Also in his Books in our time. Wash., D.C., Corsortium Press, 1972. p.292-314)

1220. _____. "Historic and artistic bindings in American libraries." (In Festschrift Ernst Kyriss. Stuttgart, Hettler, 1961. p.465-74)

1221. _____. Kurze Geschichte der Handbuchbinderei in den Vereinigten Staaten von America. Stuttgart, Hettler, 1955. 111p.

> Appeared in English as "Some notes on the history of bookbinding in the United States." American book collector 7, nos. 5-7, Jan.-Mar. 1955.

Early History to 1800

1222. Andrews, William L. "Early American bookbinding." Bookman 16:56-69, 164-75, Sept.-Oct. 1902.

1223. Dreis, Hazel. "Lancaster, Pennsylvania, bookbindings." Publications of the Bibliographical Society of America 42:119-28, 1st quarter 1948.

> Much of the article is on the work of the bindery of the Ephrata Cloister.

1224. Early American bookbindings from the collection of Michael Papantonio. N.Y., Pierpont Morgan Library with the American Antiquarian Society, Cornell and Princeton Univ. Libraries and the Univ. of Virginia Library, 1972. 89p. 61 illus.

1225. Ehrman, Albert. "Early American bookbinders." Publications of the Bibliographical Society of America 35:210-11, 3d quarter 1941.

1226. Forman, Sidney. "Simplicity and utility: examples of early American bindings." Columbia Library columns 12:23-31, Feb. 1963.

1227. French, Hannah D. "The amazing career of Andrew Barclay, Scottish bookbinder of Boston." Studies in bibliography 14:145-62. 1961.

1228. French, Hannah D. "Bookbinding in colonial America." AB bookman's weekly 58:1899-1900, 1902, 1904, 1906, Oct. 11, 1976.

1229. _____. "Bound in Boston by Henry B. Legg." Studies in bibliography 17:135-39. 1964.

1230. _____. "Caleb Buglass, binder of the proposed Book of Common Prayer, Phila., 1776." Winterthur portfolio 6:15-32. 1970.

1231. _____. "Decorated American bookbinding 1636-1820." Master's thesis, Columbia, 1939.

1232. _____. "Early American bookbinding by hand." (In Lehmann-Haupt, Hellmut, ed. Bookbinding in America. N.Y., Bowker, 1967. p.3-127)

    Appendix A contains a list of American binders 1636-1820 arranged by city and town. Appendix B contains a supplement to the Grolier Club's Catalog of ornamental leather bookbindings executed in America prior to 1850 (1907).

1233. _____. "Scottish-American bookbindings: six examples from colonial North America." Book collector 6:150-59, summer 1957.

1234. Goff, Frederick R. "German folk bindings on 'Phila' books of 1774." Gutenberg Jahrbuch 1968, p.324-30.

1235. Grolier Club, N.Y. Catalog of ornamental leather bookbindings executed in America prior to 1850. Exhibited at the Grolier Club Nov. 7 to 30, 1907. N.Y., 1907. 106p.

    Additional bindings listed by Hannah D. French in Bookbinding in America, edited by Hellmut Lehmann-Haupt.

1236. Holmes, Thomas J. "Bookbindings of John Ratcliff and Edmund Ranger, 17th century Boston bookbinders." Procs. of the American Antiquarian Society 38:31-50. 1929. Additional notes, 39:291-306. 1930.

1237. McGill, William. "Scottish bookbinders in colonial America." Publishers' circular 159:193-94, Mar. 31, 1945.

1238. Samford, C. Clement. The bookbinder in eighteenth-century Williamsburg. Williamsburg, 1959. 32p. illus.

1239. _____ and Hemphill, John M. Bookbinding in colonial Virginia. Charlottesville, Univ. Press of Virginia, 1966. 185p. illus.

1240. Spawn, Willman and Spawn, Carol. "The Aitken shop: identification of an eighteenth century bindery and its tools." Publications of the Bibliographical Society of America 57:422-37, Oct./Dec. 1963.

    Robert Aitken was an American binder in Phila.

1241. _____ and _____. "Francis Skinner, bookbinder of Newport, an eighteenth-century craftsman." Winterthur portfolio 2:47-61. 1965.

19th Century

1242. Allen, Sue. "Floral-patterned endpapers in nineteenth century American books." Winterthur portfolio 12:183-224. 1977.

1243. _____. "Machine-stamped bookbindings 1834-1860." Antiques 115:564-72, Mar. 1979.

      Contains a "Checklist of binders'signatures found on American cloth-bound books through 1860," p.571-72.

1244. _____. Victorian bookbindings; a pictorial survey. rev. ed. Chicago, Univ. of Chicago, 1976. 53p. and 3 microfiche sheets in pocket.

      Mainly British, but includes American. "List of books illustrated," p.39-53.

1245. Bowdoin, William G. "American bookbinders and their work." Independent 54:2997-3004, Dec. 18, 1902.

      Contains bindings by Otto Zahn, Stikeman, Ralph Randolph Adams, P. B. Sanford, Miss M. E. Bulkley, Florence Foote, Elizabeth G. Chapin, Peter Verburg, Miss E. G. Starr, James Pawson and James B. Nicholson, and the Club Bindery.

1246. _____. "Art in American book-bindings." Independent 52: 2963-68, Dec. 13, 1900.

      Contains bindings by Miss E. G. Starr, P. J. Pfister, Florence Foote, P. B. Sanford, Otto Zahn, Stikeman, and Dudley and Hodge.

1247. _____. "Artistic bookbinding in America." Outlook 71:254-61, May 24, 1902.

1248. Brainard, Newton C., ed. The Andrus Bindery: a history of the shop 1831-1838. Hartford, Conn., Priv. printed, The Case, Lockwood and Brainard Co., 1940. 5, 13-45p.

      About the Silas Andrus bindery in Hartford, Conn.

1249. Comparato, Frank E. "The industrialization of the American bindery." (In his Books for the millions. Harrisburg, Pa., Stackpole, 1971. p.99-259)

1250. Forman, Sidney. "Simplicity and utility; examples of early American bindings." Columbia Library columns 12:23-31, Feb. 1963.

1251. French, Hannah D. "John Roulstone's Harvard bindings." Harvard library bulletin 18:171-82, Apr. 1970.

1252. Greene, Douglas G. and Hearn, Michael P. W. W. Denslow. Mt. Pleasant, Mich., Clarke Historical Library, Central Michigan Univ., 1976. 225p. illus.

      William W. Denslow (1856-1915) was an American painter who worked for Elbert Hubbard in 1896 at the Roycroft Shop. Contains a list of his book covers, p.195-98.

1253. Holmes, Thomas J. Fine bookbinding. Rowfantia, number eight.
Read at the Rowfant Club by Thomas J. Holmes. Cleveland, Rowfant Club,
1912. 50p.

     Includes 3 photogravures of bindings by the Rowfant Bindery.

1254. Howard, Edward G. "Signed Maryland bindings." Maryland historical
magazine 62:438, Dec. 1967; 63:68, Mar. 1968; 63:313-14, Sept. 1968.

1255. Jamieson, Eleanore. "The binding styles of the gift books and
annuals." (In Faxon, Frederick W. Literary annuals and gift books; a
bibliography 1823-1903. Pinner, Middlesex, England, Private Libraries
Association, 1973. p.7-17)

1256. Koch, Robert. "Artistic books, periodicals and posters of the
"gay nineties." Art quarterly 25:370-83, winter 1962.

     Contains illustrations for 7 book covers by Otto Zahn.

1257. Lethwidge, Arnold. Bookbindings of Ralph Randolph Adams.
Greenwich, Conn., Literary Collector Press, 1904. 24p. 5 plates.

1258. Malone, Walter. "Otto Zahn and his bookbindings." Book buyer
16:122-25, Mar. 1898.

     Contains 6 of his bindings.

1259. O'Neal, David L. "Early American signed cloth bindings."
American book collector 21:27, Oct. 1970.

1260. _____. "William Swaim: prizewinning binder." American book
collector 24:30, Sept./Oct. 1973.

1261. Pennell, Elizabeth R. Charles Godfrey Leland. Boston, Houghton
Mifflin, 1906. 2 vols. plates. facs.

1262. Rogers, Joseph W. "The industrialization of American bookbinding."
M. S. thesis, School of Library Service, Columbia Univ., 1937.

1263. _____. "The rise of American edition binding." (In Lehmann-
Haupt, Hellmut, ed. Bookbinding in America. N.Y., Bowker, 1967. p.131-
85b)

1264. Saunier, Charles. "La reliure moderne." L'art décoratif no. 30:
253-63, Mar. 1901.

     Includes 3 illustrations by Sandford B. Pomeroy, American artist
     and binding decorator.

1265. Strange, Edward F. "American bookbindings." (In Modern bookbindings and their designers. N.Y., John Lane, 1900. p.47-57)

1266. Thompson, Lawrence S. "Hand bookbinding in the United States
since the Civil War." Libri 5, no. 2:97-121. 1954. Also in his Books
in our time. Wash., D.C., Consortium Press, 1972. p.267-90.

1267. Thompson, Susan O. "The arts and crafts book." (In The arts and crafts movement in America 1876-1916; an exhibition organized by the Art Museum,Princeton University and the Art Institute of Chicago. Ed. by Robert J. Clark. Princeton, Princeton Univ. Press, 1972. p.93-116)

1268. Trienens, Roger J. "Hans Breitmann's bindings." Quarterly journal of the Library of Congress 23:3-8, Jan. 1966.

> About Charles G. Leland (1824-1903), versatile American author and binder. Hans Breitman was his most successful character creation. He rebound and repaired cookbooks (39 of which are in the Library of Congress). The Phila. Museum of Art has a rather large number of his bindings.

1269. Vickery, Willis. The Rowfant Bindery. Cleveland, Priv. printed, 1928. 32p.

20th Century

1270. Chandler, Lyman. "The Roycroft Shop." Graphic arts 4:117-32, Aug. 1912.

1271. Clizbee, Azalea. "Curtis Walters." American book collector 2:124-34. 1932.

1272. Comparato, Frank E. "America: the automated line." (In Books for the millions. Harrisburg, Pa., Stackpole, 1961. p.263-96)

1273. DeFlorez, Peter. "Review of new developments in bindery equipment." Publishers' weekly 173:78-80, Apr. 14, 1958.

1274. Doebler, Paul D. "Interest high in new bindery technology." Publishers' weekly 206:26, 28, 30, Sept. 2, 1974.

1275. Eaton, Allen H. "Bookbinding." (In Handicrafts of New England. N.Y., Harper, 1949. p.262-65)

> Contains brief information about many binders in New England.

1276. Gimpel & Weitzenhoffer, N.Y. Gérard Charrière: the art of bookbinding. N.Y., 1970. 15p. 9 illus.

> Gérard Charrière (1935-) is a Swiss binder in New York City.

1277. Grolier Club, N.Y. An exhibition of some of the latest artistic bindings done at the Club Bindery, 114 West 32d Street, New York. N.Y., 1906. 47p.

> Lists 138 vols with brief description of binding.

1278. Gullans, Charles B. and Espey, John J. A checklist of trade bindings designed by Margaret Armstrong. Los Angeles, Univ. of California Library, 1968. 36p. illus. (UCLA Library Occasional papers, no. 16)

1279. Harris, Helen J. A history of Joseph Ruzicka, Inc., library book-binders, 1758-1966. Master's thesis, Univ. of North Carolina, 1966.
72 leaves.illus. (ACRL microform series no. 178).

> The thesis begins with a brief history of the early years of the
> Ruzicka bindery and continues with separate chapters on the
> history of the Baltimore and Greensboro plants, the Ruzicka family,
> the library binding at Joseph Ruzicka, Inc., growth and progress,
> and challenge of the future.

1280. Hopkins, Frederick M. "Bookbinders' problems; the future of book-binding in America depends upon an awakening of enthusiasm."
Publishers' weekly 126:507-09, Aug. 18, 1934.

1281. Hunter, Dard. "Fifty years a binder: the story of Peter Franck."
Print 4:29-36, autumn 1946.

1282. Koch, Robert. "Elbert Hubbard's Roycrofters as artist-craftsmen."
Winterthur portfolio 3:67-82. 1967.

> In 1893 Elbert Hubbard (1856-1915), American author, printer, and
> designer, formed the Roycroft Press in emulation of the Kelmscott
> Press. C. W. Youngers was head binder and Lorenz Schwartz was
> assistant binder. The article contains 2 illustrations of bind-
> ings, both supervised by Louis Kinder, a German-born binder.

1283. Myrick, Frank B. "Some new advances in bindery technology."
Publishers' weekly 193:50-51, Jan. 1, 1968.

1284. Ormond, Suzanne and Irvine, Mary E. Louisiana's art nouveau: the
crafts of the Newcomb style. Gretna, Pelican, 1976. 182p. illus.

> Contains illustrations of the work of the Newcomb Guild of
> Newcomb College in New Orleans during the period 1918 to 1936.
> Bindings by Maude Parsons, Eunice Baccich, Mireille LeBreton,
> Mary Hall Tupper, and Lilian Walther on p.104-06.

1285. Pierpont Morgan Library, N.Y. The fine bindings of Marguerite
Duprez Lahey; an exhibition at the Pierpont Morgan Library, N.Y., Nov. 7,
1951-Jan. 5, 1952. N.Y., 1951. 16p. illus.

1286. Pommer, Richard. "Gerhard Gerlach, bookbinder." Craft horizons
12:23-25, Sept. 1952.

1287. Preston, Emily. "Modern tendencies in bookbinding." Independent
69:1266-71, Dec. 8, 1910.

1288. Rose Bindery Company, Boston. The Rose Bindery; your library and
our work. Boston, 1925. 13p. plates.

1289. Roylance, Dale. "Gérard Charrière: binding as art." American
craft 40:24-27, Aug./Sept. 1980.

1290. Swift, Claire C. "Fine art of bookbinding." Outlook 90:433-40,
Oct. 24, 1908.

1291. Thayer, Lee. "The Decorative Designers: a footnote on publishing history." Publishers' weekly 164:874-78, Sept. 5, 1953.

Decorative Designers produced designs for cloth-covered books.

1292. Thompson, Elbert A. "American hand binders: Peter Franck." Bookbinding and book production 50:43-44, Nov. 1949.

1293. _____ and Thompson, Lawrence S. Fine binding in America; the story of the Club Bindery. Urban, Illinois, Phi Beta Mu, 1956. 45p. illus.

1294. Thompson, Lawrence S. "Hand bookbinding in the United States since the Civil War." Libri 5, no. 2:97-121. 1954.

Contains brief information about many binders with reference to articles and books about them. Includes plates of bindings by Robert Lunow, Harold W. Tribolet, Mrs. Sinclair Hamilton, Vida G. Benedict, Mrs. H. Richard Archer, and the Club Bindery.

1295. Weisse, Franz. "Curtis Walters: ein amerikanische Buchbinder." Archiv für Buchbinderei 34:73-75. 1934.

Yugoslavia

1296. Babic, Ljubo. "Jugoslawische Einbandkunst." Jahrbuch der Einbandkunst 1929/30, p.128-31.

1297. Janc, Zagorka. Kozni povezi srpske knjige od 12 do 19 veka. Beograd, 1974. 172p. illus.

Other Countries

1298. Eisen, Gustavus A. "The art of book covers." International studio 80:91-98, Nov. 1924.

On oriental book covers, including Syria and Egypt. Contains 2 Egyptian book covers of the 14th century.

1299. Marçais, Georges and Poinssot, Louis. Objects kairouanais ix^2 au xiii^2 siècle: reliures, verreries, cuivre et bronze, bijoux. Tunis, Tournier, 1948-52. 2 vols. illus. 60 plates. (Tunis. Direction des Antiquités et Arts. Notes et documents 11)

1300. Pierpont Morgan Library, N.Y. Central European manuscripts in the Pierpont Morgan Library. Comp. by Meta Harrsen. N.Y., 1958. 86p. 90 plates.

Contains manuscripts produced in Germany, Switzerland, Austria, Hungary, and Bohemia before 1500. Several plates, including color reproduction of the upper and lower covers of the Lindau Gospels.

1301. Quinton, J. C. "Bookbinding." (In Standard encyclopedia of Southern Africa. Cape Town, Nasou Limited, 1973. vol. 9, p.139-40)

1302. Regemorter, Berthe van. "Ethiopian bookbindings." Library 17:85-88, Mar. 1962.

1303. Ricard, Prosper. "Reliures marocaines du xiii² siècle." Hesperia 17:109-27. 1933.

1304. Thompson, Lawrence S. "Bookbindings in the Americas." Inter-American review of bibliography 7:no. 3, July-Sept. 1962. Also in Books in our time. Wash., D.C., Consortium Press, 1972. p.293-314)

1305. _____. "Introductory notes on the history of bookbinding in Spanish America." Libri 10, no. 1:10-22. 1960.

1306. Tucci, G. "Tibetan book-covers." (In Art and thought. Issued in honor of Ananda K. Coomaraswamy.... Ed. by K. Bharatha Iyer. London, Luzac, 1947. p.63-68)

8

CARE AND REPAIR OF BINDINGS

Reference Works

1307. Banks, Paul N. A selective bibliography on the conservation of research library materials. Chicago, Newberry Library, 1981.

1308. Cunha, George A. and Cunha, Dorothy G. Conservation of library materials, a manual and bibliography on the care, repair and restoration of library materials. 2d ed. Metuchen, N.J., Scarecrow Press, 1971-72. 2 vols.

1309. Dühmert, Anneliese. Buchpflege, eine Bibliographie. Stuttgart, Hettler, 1963. 209p.

1310. Morrow, Carolyn C. and Schoenly, Steven B. A conservation bibliography for librarians, archivists, and administrators. N.Y., Whitston, 1979. 271p.

1311. Swartzburg, Susan G. Preserving library materials. Metuchen, N.Y., Scarecrow Press, 1980. 282p. illus.

    Bibliography p.221-78.

General Works

1312. Banks, Paul N. "Preservation of library materials." Encyclopedia of library and information science 23:180-222. 1978.

1313. Bogardus, D. F. "Revitalization of old bindings." Pacific bindery talk 7:135-39, Apr. 1935.

1314. Bonnardot, Alfred. De la réparation des vieilles reliures. Paris, Castel, 1858. 70p.

1315. Burdett, Eric. "Repairs to books." (In The craft of bookbinding. London, David and Charles, 1975. p.331-47)

1316. Cains, Anthony. "New attitudes to conservation." (In Smith, Philip. New directions in bookbinding. London, Studio Vista, 1974. p.164-72)

1317. Cockerell, Douglas. Bookbinding and the care of books. 5th ed. London, Pitman, 1971. 345p.

1318. Cockerell, Douglas. Some notes on bookbinding. London, Oxford
Univ. Press, 1929. 105p. illus.

1319. Cockerell, Sydney M. The repairing of books. 2d ed. London,
Sheppard Press, 1960. 110p. illus.

1320. Gardner, Anthony. "The ethics of book repairs." Library 9:194-98,
Sept. 1954.

1321. Horton, Carolyn. Cleaning and preserving bindings and related
materials. 2d ed. Chicago, American Library Association, 1969. 87p.
illus.

1322. Lehmann-Haupt, Hellmut. "On the rebinding of old books." (In
Bookbinding in America. Ed. by Hellmut Lehmann-Haupt. N.Y., Bowker,
1967. p.189-283 and supplement, p.283-83ℓ)

1323. Lydenberg, Harry M. The care and repair of books. Rev. by John
Alden. 4th ed. N.Y., Bowker, 1960. 122p.

1324. Muir, David. Binding and repairing books by hand. N.Y., Arco,
1978. 120p. illus.

1325. Swartzburg, Susan G. Preserving library materials. Metuchen,
N.J., Scarecrow Press, 1980. 282p. illus.

1326. Wessel, Carl J. "Deterioration of library materials." Encyclopedia of library and information science 7:69-120. 1972.

Leather and Parchment

1327. Banks, Paul N. Treating leather bookbindings. rev. ed. Chicago,
Newberry Library, 1974. 4p.

1328. Belaya, I. K. "Softening and restauration of parchment in manuscripts and bookbindings." Restaurator 1:20-51. 1969.

1329. Innes, R. Faraday. "Causes and prevention of decay in leather."
Library Association record 1:393-99, Nov. 1934.

1330. Middleton, Bernard C. The restoration of leather bindings.
Chicago, American Library Association, 1972. 201p. illus.

1331. Plenderleith, Harold. The preservation of leather bookbindings.
London, British Museum, 1967. 32p. 4 plates.

1332. Smith, Richard D. "The preservation of leather bookbindings from
sulphuric acid deterioration." Master's paper, Univ. of Denver, 1964.

1333. U. S. Dept. of Agriculture. Leather bookbindings, how to preserve
them. By J. S. Rogers and C. W. Beebe. Wash., D.C., 1956. 8p.
(Booklet no. 398).

1334. U. S. Library of Congress. Preserving leather bookbindings.
Wash., D.C., 1975. 4p.

1335. Waterer, John W. A guide to the conservation and restoration of
objects made wholly or in part of leather. London, Bell, 1972. 60p.
illus.

1336. Wheatley, Henry B. "Leather for bookbinding." Library 2:311-20,
July 1901.

1337. Wire, George E. Leather preservation. Worcester, Mass., Common-
wealth Press, 1911. 12p.

9

STUDY OF BOOKBINDING

General Works

1338. Bogeng, Gustav A. "Der Bucheinband in seiner Entstehung und Fortbildung." Archiv für Geschichte des Buchwesens 1:3-37. 1958.

1339. Boswell, David B. "Bookbinding." (In A textbook on bibliography. London, Grafton, 1952. p.118-34)

1340. Bowers, Fredson. "Binding." (In Principles of bibliographical description. Princeton, Princeton Univ. Press, 1949. p.376-78, 446-50)

1341. Davenport, Cyril J. "Specimens of binding." (In Beautiful books. London, Methuen, 1929. p.74-105)

1342. Diehl, Edith. "The kinds of binding." Dolphin 2:131-43. 1935.

1343. Gid, D. "De l'importance de la reliure dans l'étude du livre." (In France. Centre Nationale de la Recherche Scientifique, Paris, 1972. Paléographie hébraïque médiévale. Colloque internationale. Paris, 1974. p.167-70)

1344. Loubier, Hans. "Methodische Erforschung des Bucheinbands." (In Beiträge zum Bibliotheks- und Buchwesen. Paul Schwenke zum 20. Berlin, Breslauer, 1913. p.175-84)

1345. Lüfling, Hans. "Historische Einbandkunde und Buchgeschichte." Marginalien 1972, no. 48, p.3-10.

1346. McKerrow, Ronald B. "The forms in which books have been issued to the public." (In An introduction to bibliography for literary students. Oxford, Clarendon Press, 1928. p.121-27)

1347. Pollard, Graham. "Describing medieval bookbindings." (In Medieval learning and literature, essays presented to Richard William Hunt. Ed. by J. J. G. Alexander and M. T. Gibson. Oxford, Clarendon Press, 1976. p.50-65)

1348. Rouveyre, Edouard. Connaissances nécessaires à un bibliophile accompagnées de notes critiques et documents bibliographiques. 5th ed. vol. 4. Paris, Edouard Rouveyre, 1899. 151p. illus.

> An excellent book for the student who wants to learn binding styles. Contains many illustrations. The end of the volume has samples of types of marbled paper for covers and end papers.

1349. Schlumberger, Eveline. "Les meilleurs modèles pour reconnaître les reliures du xviiie siècle." <u>Connaissances des arts</u> no. 160:63-69, June 1965.

Classification

1350. Hartzog, Martha. "Nineteenth-century cloth bindings." <u>Publications of the Bibliographical Society of America</u> 61:114-19, 2d quarter 1967.

1351. Loubier, Hans. "Versuch einer Klassifizierung der Einbände für Jean Grolier." (In <u>Bok- och biblioteks-historiska studier, tillagnade Isak Collijn.</u> Uppsala, Almqvist & Wiksell, 1925. p.421-34)

1352. Sadleir, Michael. "The nomenclature of nineteenth-century cloth grains." <u>Book collector</u> 2, no. 1:54-58. 1953.

> Appears also in the author's <u>XIX century fiction</u> (1951). See also in vol. 1 of this work for plates showing examples of binding patterns.

1353. Shalleck, Jamie K. "Identifying and classifying fine bindings." (In Fletcher, H. George, ed. <u>A miscellany for bibliophiles.</u> N.Y., Grastorf and Lang, 1979. p.127-57)

1354. Tanselle, G. Thomas. "The bibliographical description of patterns." <u>Studies in bibliography</u> 23:71-102. 1970.

1355. _____. "A system of color identification for bibliographical description." <u>Studies in bibliography</u> 20:203-34. 1967. Also in <u>Selected studies in bibliography.</u> Charlottesville, Published for the Bibliographical Society of the University of Virginia by the Univ. Press of Virginia, 1979. p.139-70)

1356. _____. "Table 9. The classification of book-cloth grains." (In Gaskell, Philip. <u>A new introduction to bibliography</u>. Oxford, Clarendon Press, 1972. p.240-41)

1357. Voge, Law and Blaylock, F. R. "Tentative expanded classification of bookbinding techniques." <u>Share your knowledge review</u> 20:12-21, May 1939.

Forgery

1358. Davenport, Cyril J. "Forgeries in bookbinding." <u>Library</u> 2:389-95. 1901.

1359. Eudel, Paul. <u>Le truquage; altérations, fraudes et contrefaçons dévoilées</u>. Paris, Librairie Molière, 1908. 419p.

1360. Harrisse, Henry. <u>Les falsifications bolognaises, reliures et livres</u>. Paris, Leclerc, 1903. 57p.

1361. Helwig, Hellmuth. Einbandfälschungen. Imitation, Fälschung und
Verfälschung historischer Bucheinbände. Stuttgart, Hettler, 1968. 98p.
illus.

1362. Neuberger, Albert. Echt oder Fälschung? Leipzig, Voigtlander,
1924. 206p. illus.

1363. Nixon, Howard M. "Binding forgeries." (In 6th International
Congress of Bibliophiles, Vienna, 1969. Vorträge. Vienna, 1971.
p.69-83)

1364. _____. "Bookbinding fakes and forgeries. A lecture given to
the Thiele-Stichting, Amsterdam on March 23, 1970." (unverified)

1365. Schreiber, Heinrich. "Einbandfälschungen und ihre Literatur."
Sankt Wiborada 5:97-100. 1938.

10

AUDIOVISUAL AIDS

1366. Allen, Sue. Victorian bookbindings; a pictorial survey. rev. ed. Chicago, Univ. of Chicago Press, 1976. 53p. 3 microfiche sheets in pocket.

1367. A book by its cover. Iowa State Univ., 1968. color film. 12 minutes.

1368. Bookbinders. AFL/CIO, 1959. black and white film. 14 minutes.

1369. Fritz and Trudi Eberhardt. Cinema Group Productions, 1970. color film. 27 minutes.

1370. Fürstenberg, Jean. Le grand siècle en France et ses bibliophiles. Hamburg, Hauswedell, 1972. 160p. and 60 slides of bindings.

1371. French bookbinding from the 16th century to the present. Society for French-American Cultural Services and Educational Aid, 1959. 32 slides with text.

1372. Shannon, Faith and Cains, Tony. The bookbinder's art. 50 slides on technique and 30 on finished bindings. Commentary by Lucinda Gane. Produced by the Crafts Council in 1979.

11

BOOKPLATES

Reference Works

1373. Arellanes, Audrey S. Bookplates; a selected annotated bibliography of the periodical literature. Detroit, Gale Research, 1971. 474p.

1374. British Museum. Dept. of Prints and Drawings. Catalog of British and American bookplates bequeathed to the Trustees of the British Museum by A. W. Franks. London, 1903-04. 3 vols.

1375. Fowler, Harry A. Directory of bookplate artists, with notes concerning their work. 2d ed. Kansas City, Alfred Fowler, 1921. 29p.

1376. Fuller, George W., ed. A bibliography of bookplate literature edited with a foreword by George W. Fuller, bibliographic work by Verna B. Grimm. Spokane, Wash., Public Library, 1926. 151p.

1377. Oyen, Anthonie A. Vosterman van. Bibliographie des ouvrages, plaquettes, articles de revues et de journaux sur les ex libris. Arnhem, 1910. 23p.

1378. Prescott, Winward. "Checklist of bookplate literature." (In Ward, Harry P. Some American college bookplates. Columbus, Ohio, 1915. p.403-57)

1379. _____. A bibliography of bookplate literature. Princeton, N.J., American Bookplate Society, 1914. 70p.

1380. Rödel, Klaus. Bibliografi over europaeiske kunstneres exlibris. Copenhagen, Exlibristen, 1971. 46p.

1381. Vils Pedersen, Jorgen. List of exlibris literature: articles, books, catalogs, maps and graphic. Copenhagen, The Compiler, 1976. 80p.

General Works

1382. Andrews, Irene D. Owners of books. Washington, Bruin Press, 1936. 271p. illus.

A book about the owners of bookplates and the men who made them. Contains many illustrations of bookplates.

1383. Barnett, Percy N. Armorial book-plates; their romantic origin and artistic development. Sydney, Priv. printed, 1932. 172p. illus.

1384. Beddingham, Philip. Concerning bookplates. North Harrow (England), Private Libraries Association, 1960. 14p. illus.

1385. Beels, C. H. and Peskens, J. T. Heraldiek in het exlibris. Amsterdam, Wereldbibliotheek, 1967. 80p. illus.

1386. Hamilton, Walter. Dated book-plates...with a treatise on their origin and development. London, Black, 1895. 225p. about 100 illus. plates.

1387. Hardy, William J. Book plates. 2d ed. London, Paul, Trench, Trübner, 1897. 240p. 43 plates.

1388. Hedegaard, E. O. Militaere bogejermaerker. Exlibris. Helsinger, Andersen, 1967. 208p. illus.

1389. Horodisch, Abraham. Miniatur exlibris. Amsterdam, Erasmus, 1966. 95, 28p. illus.

1390. Johnson, Fridolf. A treasury of bookplates: from the Renaissance to the present. N.Y., Dover, 1977. 151p. 761 illus.

1391. Jones, Louise S. The human side of bookplates. Los Angeles, Ritchie Press, 1951. 158p. illus.

1392. Labouchere, Norna. Ladies' bookplates. London, Bell, 1895. 358p. illus. plates.

1393. Mason, Stanley. "Ex libris, a dying art form." Graphis 29, no. 166:190-97. 1973-74.

1394. Modern book-plates and their designers. Studio, special winter no. 1898-99. 78p. illus.

1395. Schickell, Edward H. Bookplates for libraries. Roger Beacham, 1968. pages?

1396. Severin, Mark and Reid, Anthony. Engraved bookplates, European exlibris 1950-1970. Pinner, England, Private Libraries Association, 1972. 176p. chiefly facsimiles.

1397. Stone, Wilbur M. Some children's book-plates. Governeur, N.Y., Brothers of the Book, 1901. 39p. plates.

1398. _____. Women designers of book-plates. N.Y., Published for the Triptych by R. R. Beam, 1902. 35 plates.

1399. Teall, Gardner. "A revival of interest in the bookplate." International studio 86:71-76, Jan. 1927.

Art and Technique

1400. Johnson, Fridolf. "The art of the bookplate." American artist 29:48-53, May 1965.

1401. Severin, Mark F. Making a bookplate. London, Studio Publications, 1949. 88p. illus.

1402. Stone, Wilbur M., ed. Book-plates of today, and the architect as a bookplate designer by Willis Steell. N.Y., Wessels, 1902. 80p. 90 illus.

1403. Vinycomb, John. On the processes for the production of ex libris. London, 1894. 12, 96p. illus. 22 plates.

France

1404. Guigard, Joannis. Nouvel armorial du bibliophile. Paris, Rondeau, 1890. 2 vols. illus.

1405. Hamilton, Walter. French book-plates. 2d ed. London, Bell, 1896. 360p. illus.

1406. Meyer-Noirel, G. Bibliographie de l'ex libris français 1872-1977. Frederikshavn, Exlibristen, 1979. 220p. illus.

1407. Olivier, Eugène et al. Manuel de l'amateur de reliures armoriées françaises. Paris, Bosse, 1924-38. 30 vols. illus.

1408. Uzanne, Octave. "French book-plates." Studio, special winter no. 1898-99, p.47-58.

1409. Valotaire, Marcel. L'art de l'ex-libris en France. Paris, Daragon, 1921. 40p. illus.

1410. Wiggishoff, Jacques C. Dictionnaire des dessinateurs et graveurs d'exlibris français. Paris, Société Française des Collectionneurs d'Ex-libris, 1915. 278p. illus. plates.

Germany

1411. Braungart, Richard. Neue deutsche AKT-exlibris. Munich, 1924. 168p. illus.

1412. Laut, Hans. Exlibris-Kunst aus dem deutschsprachigen Gebiet. Berlin, Hoffmann, 1955. 154p. illus.

1413. Leininger-Westerburg, Karl Emich Count zu. German book-plates. Tr. by G. R. Dennis. London, 1901. 531p. illus.

1414. Schwencke, Johan. Het exlibris in Duitsland. Amsterdam, Westereld-Bibliotheek, 1963. 61p. illus. facs.

1415. Singer, Hans W. "German bookplates." Studio, special winter no., 1898-99, p.63-68.

1416. Warnecke, Friedrich. Die deutschen Bücherzeichen. Berlin, Stargardt, 1899. 255p. illus. 27 plates.

Great Britain

1417. Bookplate Society, London. Bookplate designers 1925-1975. London, Private Libraries Association, 1976. 50p. illus. plates (exhibit catalog)

1418. British Museum. Dept. of Prints and Drawings. Catalog of British and American book plates bequeathed to the Trustees of the British Museum by Sir A. W. Franks. London, 1903-04. 3 vols.

1419. Castle, Egerton. English bookplates ancient and modern. London, Bell, 1894. 352p. illus. plates.

1420. Fincham, Henry W. Artists and engravers of British and American book plates. London, Trench, Trübner, 1897. 135p. illus. plates.

1421. Lee, Brian N. Early printed book labels; a catalogue of dated personal labels and gift labels printed in Britain to the year 1760. Pinner, England, Private Libraries Association for the Bookplate Society, 1976. 185p. illus.

1422. Slater, John H. Bookplates and their value; English and American plates. London, H. Grant, 1898. 241p.

1423. Viner, G. H. "The origin and evolution of the book-plate." Library 1:39-44, June 1946.

1424. White, Gleeson. "British book-plates." Studio, special winter no. 1898-99, p.3-44.

Italy

1425. Gelli, Jocopo. Gli ex libris italiani. Milan, Hoepli, 1930. 500p. illus.

1426. Schwencke, Johan. Het exlibris in Italië. Amsterdam, Wereld-bibliotheek, 1949. 48p.

Jewish

1427. Goodman, Philip. "American Jewish bookplates." Publications of the American Jewish Historical Society 45:129-216, Mar. 1956.

1428. _____. "Bookplates." Encyclopedia Judaica 4:columns 1219-20. 1971.

1429. _____. Illustrated essays on Jewish bookplates. N.Y., KTAV Publishing House, 1971. 196p. illus.

1430. _____. "Jewish bookplate literature; an annotated bibliography." (In Berlin, Charles. Studies in Jewish bibliography and history and literature in honor of I. Edward Kiev. N.Y., KTAV Publishing House, 1971. p.113-31)

1431. _____. "Love of books as revealed in Jewish bookplates." Jewish book annual 1954, p.77-90.

1432. Habermann, Abraham M. Tave sefer yehudijim. 1972? 121p. 165 facs.

Netherlands

1433. Koolwijk, Th.F. van and Rödel, Klaus. Bibliografi over hollandsk exlibrislitteratur 1890-1975. Frederikshavn, Exlibristen, 1977. 55p. plates.

1434. Nielsen, A. C. Latijnse zinspreuken op Nederlandse boekmarken. Amsterdam, Harms, 1952. 60p. illus.

1435. Oyen, Anthonie A. Vosterman van. Les dessinateurs neerlandais d'exlibris. Arnhem, 1910. 40, 10p.

1436. Schwencke, Johan. Exlibriskunde. Amsterdam, Wereldbibliotheek, 1947. 170p. illus.

      Covers Netherlands and Belgium with a bibliography of bookplates for 1837-1946.

1437. _____. Het beeld van het Nederlandse exlibris 1880-1960. Amsterdam, Harms, 1960. 78p. illus.

1438. Veth, D. Giltay. Dutch book plates; a selection of modern woodcuts and wood engravings. N.Y., Golden Griffin Book Arts, 1950. 53p. 83 illus.

Portugal

1439. Lima, Mathias. Super-libros portuguezes ineditos. Porto, Machado, 1927. 145p.

1440. Schwencke, Johan. Het exlibris in Spanje and Portugal. Amsterdam,
Wereldbibliotheek, 1955. 45p. illus.

Russia

1441. Ekslibrysy ukrainskykh khudozhnykov. Kiev, 1977. 246p. chiefly
illus.

1442. Minaev, Evgenii N. Exlibris (translated title). Moscow, Kniga,
1970. 238p. illus.

1443. Mitrokhin, Dmitri I. et al. Knizhnye znaki russkikh khudozhnikov.
1922. 238p. illus. 55 plates.

1444. Tychna, Anatol and Shmatau, Viktor. Belaruski knizhny znak.
Mink, Belarus, 1975. 126p. illus.

Spain

1445. Schwencke, Johan. Het libris in Spanje and Portugal. Amsterdam,
Wereldbibliotheek, 1955. 45p. illus.

1446. Vindel, Francisco. Ensayo de un catálogo de ex-libris ibero-
americanos, siglos xvi-xix. Madrid, 1952. 2 vols.

United States

1447. Allen, Charles D. American book-plates; a guide to their study
with examples. N.Y., Blom, 1968. 437p. illus. (reprint of 1905
edition)

1448. _____. A classified list of early American book-plates with a
brief description of the principal styles and a note as to the prominent
engravers. To accompany an exhibition at the Grolier Club, 1894. N.Y.,
Grolier Club, 1894. 38p. illus.

1449. Borneman, Henry S. Pennsylvania German bookplates; a study.
Phila., Pennsylvania German Society, 1953. 169p. illus.

1450. Bowdoin, William G. The rise of the bookplate. N.Y., Wessels,
1901. 207p. illus.

    Contains a list of American designers and engravers.

1451. Fincham, Henry W. Artists and engravers of British and American
bookplates. London, Paul, Trench, Trübner, 1897. 135p. illus. plates.

1452. Goodhue, Bertram G. Book decorations. N.Y., Grolier Club, 1931.
82p.

1453. Harding, Dorothy S. "Contemporary bookplates." _American magazine of art_ 25:219-28, Oct. 1932.

1454. Law, Henry I. _Delaware bookplates_. Wash., D.C., Bruin Press, 1940. 55p. illus.

1455. Lichtenstein, Richard C. "American book-plates and their engravers." _Journal of the Ex Libris Society_ 1:37-46, Sept. 1891.

1456. Metzdorf, Robert F. _Index to yearbooks of the American Society of Bookplate Collectors and Designers 1923-1950_. Sewanee, Tenn., 1952.

1457. Slater, John H. _Book plates and their value; English and American plates_. London, H. Grant, 1898. 241p.

1458. Vail, Robert W. "Seventeenth century American book labels." _Publications of the American Antiquarian Society_ 43:304-16, Oct. 1933.

1459. Ward, Harry P. _Some American college bookplates...._ Columbus, Champlin Press, 1915. 482p. illus.

1460. Weitenkampf, Frank. "The book-plate." (In _American graphic art_. new ed. N.Y., Macmillan, 1924. p.251-65)

Other Countries

1461. Björkblom, Carl et al. _Svensk exlibris bibliografi_. Stockholm, 1939. 44p.

1462. Schwencke, Johan. _Het exlibris in die skandinavische landen_. Amsterdam, Wereldbibliotheek, 1953. 48p. illus.

1463. Shimo, Taro. _Japanske exlibris_. Rudkobing, Forlaget Grafolio, 1965. 64p. illus.

1464. Vindel, Francisco. _Ensayo de un catálogo de ex-libris ibero-americanos, siglos xvi-xix_. Madrid, 1952. 2 vols.

Includes Spain and Spanish America.

Study of Bookplates

1465. Adams, Frederick B. _The uses of provenance_. Berkeley, School of Librarianship, Univ. of California, 1969. 26p.

1466. Bowdoin, William G. _The rise of the book-plate...._ N.Y., Wessels, 1901. 207p. plates.

Contains a chapter on the study and arrangement of bookplates by Henry Blackwell.

1467. Eräniemi, Olavi. Exlibrikset harrasteena. Helsinki, Suomen Exlibrisyhdistys, 1972. 32p.

1468. Fowler, Harry A. Bookplates for beginners. Kansas City, A. Fowler, 1922. 48p. illus.

The author is also known as Alfred Fowler.

1469. Lee, Brian N. "The authenticity of bookplates." Book collector 30:62-73, spring 1981.

1470. _____. "Problem for the bookplate collector." Private library 6:123-32, autumn 1973.

1471. Warren, J. Leicester (Lord de Tabley). Guide to the study of bookplates. London, John Pearson, 1880. 238p. illus. 2d, corrected ed., edited by Eleanor Leighton in 1900. Reprinted by Van Heusden in Amsterdam in 1975.

12
BOOK JACKETS

General Works

1472. "The experts discuss book jackets." American artist 5:22-25, Mar. 1941.

1473. Floud, Peter and Rosner, Charles. "Book jacket comes of age; exhibition at Victoria and Albert Museum." Graphis no. 29:14-25. 1950.

1474. Gebrauchsgraphik. Munich, F. Bruckmann, 1929-71. New title: Novum gebrauchsgraphik, 1972 to date.

Contains articles about book jackets and their designers.

1475. Graphis annual. Zurich, Graphis Press, 1952/53-

Each issue contains a section on book covers and dust jackets.

1476. Petroski, Henry. "Dust jacket dilemmas." Prairie schooner 53:328-33, winter 1979/80.

1477. Somerfeldt, Carolyn R. "Book jacket, its history, commentary and critical evaluation." MSLS, Southern Connecticut State College, 1965. 104p.

1478. Stephen, George A. "Publishers' book jackets." Penrose annual 26:57-66. 1924.

1479. Tanselle, G. Thomas. "Dust-jackets, blurbs and bibliography." Library 26:91-134, June 1971.

1480. Tedesco, Anthony P. The relationship between illustration and type in books and book jackets. Brooklyn, McKibbin, 1948. 32p. illus.

1481. Tillmann, Curt. Sammlerglueck mit Zeitschriften und Buchumschlägen. 2d ed. Munich, Heimeran, 1954. 48p.

1482. Weidemann, Kurt, ed. Buchumschläge und Schallplattenhüllen. Teufen (Switzerland), Wiggli, 1969. 149p. illus. plates (Text in German, English, and French)

Published also by Praeger in New York City in 1969 under the title Book jackets and record covers; an international survey.

1483. Zurich. Kunstgewerbemuseum. Internationale Ausstellung der Buchumschlag, Veranstaltet vom Victoria und Albert Museum. London, 3 Feb. bis 4 Marz 1951. Zurich, 1951. 55p. plates.

Design

1484. Brabbins, Oliver. "Book jacket." Artist 57:114-18, July 1959.

1485. Brown, Gregory. "Book jacket design." Penrose annual 38:30-32. 1936.

1486. Coleman, Morris. "Design and creation of book jackets." American artist 18:32-36, Jan. 1954.

1487. Jennett, Seán. "The bookjacket." (In The making of books. N.Y., Pantheon, 1951. p.429-46)

1488. Kenyon, Ley. "Art of the book jacket." Artist 44:8-10, Sept. 1952; 44:36-38, Oct. 1952; 44:54-57, Nov. 1952.

1489. Ogg, Oscar. "Non-illustrative book jackets." American artist 13:44-48, Sept. 1949.

1490. Rosner, Charles. The art of the book jacket. London, Published for the Victoria and Albert Museum by HMSO, 1949. 12p.

1491. _____. "The book jacket : first principles." Penrose annual 44:44-47. 1950.

History

1492. Baer, Leo. Mit Holzschnitten verzierte Buchumschläge des XV und XVI Jahrhunderts. Frankfurt, Baer, 1923. 13 leaves.

1493. _____, ed. Holzschnitte auf Buchumschlägen aus dem XV und der ersten Hälfte Jahrhunderts. Strassburg, Heitz, 1936. 11p. mounted plates.

1494. Barber, Giles. "Continental paper wrappers and publishers bindings in the 18th century." American book collector 24:37-48. 1975.

1495. Fenton, Edward. "Some notes on the history of the book jacket." Publishers' weekly 159:899-902, Feb. 10, 1951.

1496. Jackson, William A. "Printed wrappers of the fifteenth and eighteenth centuries." Harvard library bulletin 6:313-21, autumn 1952.

1497. Marbach. Schiller-NationalMuseum. Deutsches Literaturarchiv. Buchumschläge 1900-1950. Aus der Sammlung Curt Tillman. Munich, Kosel, 1971. 234p. illus.

   The catalog was done by Walter Scheffler and Gertrud Fiege.

1498. Rosner, Charles. The growth of the book jacket. Cambridge, Harvard Univ. Press, 1954. 74p. 226 illus.

Czechoslovakia

1499. Cheronnet, Louis. "Quelques couvertures de livres tchéco-slo-
vaques." Art et décoration 56:113-16, Oct. 1929.

1500. Evenhöh, Ludwig. "Buchumschläge aus der Tschechoslowakei."
Gebrauchsgraphik 35:54-56, Feb. 1964.

Germany

1501. Schauer, Georg K. Kleine Geschichte des deutschen Buchumschläges
im 20. Jahrhundert...aus der Sammlung Curt Tillmann. Königstein im
Taunus, Langewiesche, 1962. 47p. illus.

1502. Spohn, Jürgen. "German book jackets." Novum Gebrauchsgraphik
43:2-9, Sept. 1972.

1503. Willberg, H. P. "German book jackets." Gebrauchsgraphik
41:6-17, Sept. 1970.

1504. Wills, Franz H. "Book jackets from the GDR." Gebrauchsgraphik
42:50-55, Aug. 1971.

Great Britain

1505. Ashworth, Wilfred. "Book jackets." British book news no. 315:
797-800, Nov. 1966.

1506. Grimsditch, Herbert B. "British book wrappers." Studio 92:17-21.
1926.

1507. Reavell, Cynthia. "A look at book jackets." Bookseller, May 9,
1981, p.1668-69.

1508. Rosner, Charles. "English book jackets." Graphis 2:136-44.
1946.

1509. Sitwell, Sacheverell. A note for bibliophiles. Badby, The Author,
1976. 15p. facs.

United States

1510. American Institute of Graphic Arts. 1964 paperbacks U.S.A.; an
exhibition of covers and 30 complete books. N.Y., 1965. 1 vol. (unpaged)
131 illus.

1511. Book Jacket Designers Guild. Annual exhibition. N.Y., 1948-

1512. "Cover story: book jackets, 1962." <u>Publishers' weekly</u> 183:90-95,
March 4, 1963.

      Book jacket design competition sponsored by Turck and Reinfeld,
      N.Y. printers.

1513. "Designers of book jackets." <u>Publishers' weekly</u> 161:1096-98,
Mar. 1, 1952; 162:568-71, Aug. 2, 1952.

1514. Freiman, Ray. "Look of apparent newness in books and their
jackets." <u>Publishers' weekly</u> 155:45-48, Jan. 1, 1949.

1515. Gore, Gary. "Symbolism in university press jacket design."
<u>Publishers' weekly</u> 187:92-94, Jan. 4, 1965.

1516. Hamilton, Russel D. "Eight years of book jacket design; first
exhibition of Book Jacket Designers Guild." <u>Publishers' weekly</u> 153:
2542-44, June 19, 1948.

1517. Hilten, Theodor. "Amerikanische Buchumschläge." <u>Gebrauchsgraphik</u>
35:2-11, Mar. 1964.

1518. Kohn, John. "Some notes on dust jackets." <u>Publishers' weekly</u>
132:1732-35, Oct. 30, 1937.

1519. MacMurray, Frances T. "The book jacket in America, its history
and use." Master's thesis, Catholic University of America, 1968. 97p.

1520. Pitz, Henry C. "Book jackets of today." <u>American artist</u>
12:49-53, Apr. 1948.

1521. Salter, George. "American book jackets, 4th annual exhibition."
<u>Graphis</u> no. 38:414-21. 1951. (Book Jacket Designers Guild Exhibition)

1522. _____. "Book jacket designs 1940-1947." <u>Print</u> 6, no. 1:13-23.
1948.

1523. "71 outstanding book jackets in Turck and Reinfeld contest."
<u>Publishers' weekly</u> 187:112-16, Mar. 1, 1965.

1524. Tedesco, Anthony P. "Type and illustration in book jackets."
<u>Publishers' weekly</u> 155:54-57, Jan. 1, 1949.

Other Countries

1525. Alexandre, Arsene. "French posters and book covers."
<u>Scribner's magazine</u> 17:603-14, May 1895.

1526. Heussner, Carl. "Brasilianische Buchumschläge." <u>Gebrauchsgraphik</u>
32:42-45, Sept. 1961.

1527. Plata, Walter. "Hungarian book art." <u>Gebrauchsgraphik</u> 40:40-51,
June 1969.

CHECKLIST OF TITLES
FOR A UNIVERSITY LIBRARY

Allen, Sue. Victorian bookbindings; a pictorial survey. Chicago, Univ.
of Chicago Press, 1976. 53p. 2 microfiche sheets in pocket.

Arnold, Thomas W. and Grohmann, Adolph. The Islamic book. N.Y.,
Harcourt, Brace, 1929. 130p.

Banister, Manly M. Bookbinding as a handcraft. N.Y., Sterling, 1975.
160p.

Béraldi, Henri. La reliure du xix⁺siècle. Paris, Conquet, 1895-97.
4 vols.

Bibliotheca Corviniana; the library of King Matthias of Hungary. Shannon,
Irish Univ. Press, 1969. 398p.

Bodleian Library. Fine bindings 1500-1700 from Oxford libraries; catalog
of an exhibition. Oxford, 1968. 144p.

Bogeng, Gustav A. Deutsche Einbandkunst in ersten Jahrzehnt des zwanzigsten Jahrhunderts. Halle, 1911. xxxiip. 78 pages of illus.

_____. Die grossen bibliophilen! Geschichte der Büchersammler und
ihrer Sammlungen. Leipzig, Seeman, 1922. 3 vols.

British Museum. Bookbindings from the library of Jean Grolier; a loan
exhibition 23 Sept.-31 Oct. 1965. London, 1965. 75p.

Burdett, Eric. The craft of bookbinding. Newton Abbot, David and
Charles, 1975. 400p.

Carter, John. Binding variants in English publishing 1820-1900. London,
Constable, 1932. 172p.

_____. More binding variants. London, Constable, 1938. 52p.

_____. Publisher's cloth; an outline history of publisher's binding
in England 1820-1900. N.Y., Bowker, 1935. 52p.

Clough, Eric A. Bookbinding for librarians. London, Association of
Assistant Librarians, 1957. 204p.

Cobden-Sanderson, Thomas J. Four lectures. Ed. by John Dreyfus.
San Francisco, Book Club of California, 1974. 105p.

Cockerell, Douglas. Bookbinding and the care of books. 5th ed. London,
Pitman, 1953. 345p.

Comparato, Frank S. Books for the millions. Harrisburg, Stackpole, 1971. 374p.

Craig, Maurice J. Irish bookbindings 1600-1800. London, Cassell, 1954. 47p.

Crauzat, Ernest de. La reliure française de 1900 à 1925. Paris, 1932. 2 vols.

Culot, Paul. Jean Claude Bozérian, un monument de l'ornement dans la reliure de France. Brussels, Speeckaert, 1979. 107p.

Danish eighteenth century bindings 1730-1780. With an introduction by Sofus Larsen and Anker Kyster. Copenhagen, Levin and Munksgaard, 1930. 52p.

Darley, Lionel S. Introduction to bookbinding. London, Faber and Faber, 1965. 118p.

Davenport, Cyril J. Cameo book-stamps figured and described. London, Edward Arnold, 1911. 207p.

_____. English heraldic book-stamps. London, Constable, 1909. 450p.

Davies, Hugh W., ed. Catalogue of early French books in the library of C. Fairfax Murray. London, Holland Press, 1961. 2 vols. (Reprint of 1910 ed.)

_____. Catalogue of early German books of C. Fairfax Murray. London, Holland Press, 1961. 2 vols. (Reprint of 1913 ed.)

Devauchelle, Roger. La reliure en France de ses origines à nos jours. Paris, Rousseau-Girard, 1959-61. 3 vols.

Deville, Etienne. La reliure française. Paris, Van Oest, 1930-31. 2 vols.

Diehl, Edith. Bookbinding, its background and technique. N.Y., Rinehart, 1946. 2 vols.

Dubois d'Enghien, Hector. La reliure en Belgique au 19e siècle. Brussels, Leclerc, 1954. 251p.

Duff, Edward G. The English provincial printers, stationers and book-binders to 1557. Cambridge, Univ. Press, 1912. 153p.

_____. Printers, stationers and bookbinders of Westminster and London from 1476 to 1535. Cambridge, Univ. Press, 1906. 256p.

Dühmert, Anneliese. Buchpflege; eine bibliographie. Stuttgart, Hettler, 1963. 209p.

Early American bookbindings from the collection of Michael Papantonio. N.Y., Pierpont Morgan Library with the American Antiquarian Society, Cornell and Princeton Univ. libraries and the Univ. of Virginia Library, 1972. 89p.

Festschrift Ernst Kyriss. Stuttgart, Hettler, 1961. 496p.

Foot, Mirjam M. The Henry Davis gift: a collection of bindings. vol. 1:
    Studies in the history of bookbinding. London, British Library,
    1978. 352p.

Fourny, Roger. Manuel de reliure. Paris, Librairie Polytechnique
    Béranger, Départ. Technique des Presses de la Cité, 1965. 283p.

Fürstenberg, Jean. Le grand siècle en France et ses bibliophiles.
    Hamburg, Hauswedell, 1972. 160p. and 60 slides of bindings.

Glaister, Geoffrey A. Glaister's glossary of the book. 2d ed. Berkeley,
    Univ. of California Press, 1979. 551p.

Goldschmidt, Ernst P. Gothic and Renaissance bookbindings. London,
    Benn, 1928. 2 vols.

Grautoff, Otto. Die Entwicklung der modernen Buchkunst in Deutschland.
    Leipzig, Seeman, 1901. 219p.

Gruel, Léon. Manuel historique et bibliographique de l'amateur de
    reliures. Paris, Gruel and Engelmann, 1887-1905. 2 vols.

Haemmerle, Albert and Hirsch, Olga. Buntpapier. 2d ed. Munich,
    Callwey, 1977. 255p.

Halfer, Joseph. Die Fortschritte der Marmorierkunst. 2d ed. Mit
    Anhang: Verzierung der Buchschnitte. Stuttgart, W. Leo, 1891.
    224p. (English translation in 1893 by Herman Dieck)

Harrod, Leonard M. The librarians' glossary. 4th ed. London, Deutsch,
    1977. 903p.

Hedberg, Arvid. Stockholms bokbindare 1460-1880. Stockholm, 1949-60.
    2 vols.

Helwig, Hellmuth. Das deutsche Buchbinder-Handwerk; Handwerks- und
    Kulturgeschichte. Stuttgart, Hiersemann, 1962-65. 2 vols.

_____. Einbandfälschungen. Stuttgart, Hettler, 1968. 98p.

_____. Handbuch der Einbandkunde. Hamburg, Maximilian-Gesellschaft,
    1953-55. 3 vols.

Herbst, Hermann. Bibliographie der Buchbinderei Literatur. Leipzig,
    Hiersemann, 1933. 169p.

Hobson, Anthony R. Apollo and Pegasus; an inquiry into the formation
    and dispersal of a Renaissance library. Amsterdam, Philo Press-
    Van Heusden, 1975. 250p.

Hobson, Geoffrey D. Bindings in Cambridge libraries; seventy-two plates
    with notes. Cambridge, Univ. Press, 1929. 179p.

_____. English binding before 1500. Cambridge, Univ. Press, 1929.
    58p.

Hobson, Geoffrey D. Maioli, Canevari and others. London, Benn, 1926.
     178p.

_____. Les reliures à la fanfare. 2d ed. Amsterdam, Van Heusden,
     1970. 151, 17p.

Holme, Charles, ed. The art of the book; a review of some recent
     European and American work in typography, page decoration, and bind-
     ing. London, Studio, 1914. 276p.

Horne, Herbert P. The binding of books; an essay in the history of gold-
     tooled bindings. London, Paul, Trench, Trübner, 1894. 224p. 2d ed.,
     rev. and corrected, 1915.

Horton, Carolyn. Cleaning and preserving bindings and related materials.
     2d ed. Chicago, American Library Association, 1969. 87p.

Howe, Ellic. A list of London bookbinders 1648-1815. London, Bibli-
     ographical Society, 1950. 105p.

Hunt Institute for Botanical Documentation. The tradition of fine bind-
     ing in the 20th century. Pittsburgh, Hunt Institute and Davis and
     Warde, 1979. 129p. (exhibit catalog)

Hunyady, József. A magyar könyvkötes müvészete a Mohácsi vészig.
     Budapest, Attila-Nyomda, 1937. 111p.

Jamieson, Eleanore. English embossed bindings 1825-1850. Cambridge,
     Univ. Press, 1972. 95p.

Johnson, Arthur W. The Thames and Hudson manual of bookbinding. London,
     Thames and Hudson, 1981. 224p.

Kersten, Paul. Das Goldschnittmachen.2d ed. Halle, Knapp, 1936. 32p.

_____. Der exakte Bucheinband. Halle, Knapp, 1909. 177p.

Koroknay, Eva S. Magyar reneszánsz könyvkötések kolostori és polgari
     mühelyek. Budapest, Akadémiai Kiadó, 1973. 125p.

Kyriss, Ernst. Katalog historischer Einbände des 11 bis 20 Jahrhunderts
     aus der Württembergischen Landesbibliothek. Stuttgart, 1955. 48p.

_____. Verzierte gotische Einbände im alten deutschen Sprachgebiet.
     Suttgart, Hettler, 1951-58. 4 vols.

Kyster, Anker. Bookbindings in the public collections of Denmark.
     vol. 1: The Royal Library, Copenhagen. Copenhagen, Levin and
     Munksgaard, 1938. 128p.

Lehmann-Haupt, Hellmuth, ed. Bookbinding in America. N.Y., Bowker,
     1967. 293p.

Lexikon des Buchwesens. Hrsg. von Joachim Kirchner. Stuttgart,
     Hiersemann, 1952-56. 4 vols.

Lima, Matias. Encadernadores portugueses; notulas biographicas e criticas. Porto, 1956. 216p.

Lindt, Johann. Berner Einbände, Buchbinder und Buchdrucker. Bern,
Schweizerisches Gutenbergmuseum, 1969. 214p.

López Serrano, Matilde. Biblioteca de Palacio: encuadernaciones.
Madrid, Aguado, 1950. 181p.

_____. La encuadernación española; breve historia. Madrid, Asocia-
cion de Bibliotecarios, Archivos y Arquelogos, 1972. 146p.

Loring, Rosamond. Decorated book papers. 2d ed. Ed. by Philip Hofer.
Cambridge, Harvard Univ. Press, 1952. 171p.

Loubier, Hans. Der Bucheinband von seinen Anfängen bis zum Ende des 18.
Jahrhunderts. 2d ed. Leipzig, Klinkhardt and Biermann, 1926. 272p.

Lydenberg, Harry M. and Archer, John. The care and repair of books. Rev.
by John Alden. N.Y., Bowker, 1960. 122p.

McLean, Ruari. Victorian book design and colour printing. 2d ed. London,
Faber and Faber, 1972. 241p.

_____. Victorian publishers' bookbindings in cloth and leather.
London, Gordon Fraser, 1974. 160p.

Mansfield, Edgar. Modern design in bookbinding work. London, Peter
Owen, 1966. 119p.

Marinis, Tammaro de. La biblioteca napolitana dei re d'Aragona. Milan,
1947-52. 4 vols. supp., 1969. 2 vols.

_____. Die italienischen Renaissance-Einbände der Bibliothek
Fürstenberg. Hamburg, Maximilian-Gesellschaft, 1966. 190p.

_____. La legatura artistica in Italia nei secoli xv e xvi.
Florence, Fratelli Alinari, Instituto di Edizioni Artistiche, 1960.
3 vols.

Mazal, Otto. Europäische Einbandkunst aus Mittelalter und Neuzeit.
270 Einbände der Oesterreichischen Nationalbibliothek.   Graz,
Akademische Druck- und Verlagsanstalt, 1970. 94p.

Mejer, Wolfgang. Bibliographie der Buchbinderei-Literatur. Leipzig,
Hiersemann, 1925. 208p.

Michel, Marius. L'ornementation des reliures modernes. Paris, 1889.
78p.

Michon, Louis M. Les reliures mosaïques du xviiie siècle. Paris,
Société de la Reliure Originale, 1956. 125p.

Mick, Ernst W. Altes Buntpapiere. Dortmund, Harenberg, 1979. 175p.

Middleton, Bernard C. A history of English craft bookbinding technique.
N.Y., Hafner, 1963. 307p.

Middleton, Barnard C. The restoration of leather bindings. Chicago, American Library Association, 1972. 201p.

Mitchell, William S. A history of Scottish bookbinding 1432 to 1650. Edinburgh, Oliver and Boyd, 1955. 150p.

Morrow, Carolyn C. and Schoenly, Steven B. A conservation bibliography for librarians, archivists, and administrators. N.Y., Whitston, 1979. 271p.

Needham, Paul. Twelve centuries of bookbindings 400-1600. N.Y., Pierpont Morgan Library, Oxford Univ. Press, 1979. 338p.

Nielsen, Carl P. and Berg, Rasmus. Denmarks bogbinders gennen 400 aar. Copenhagen, 1926. 273p.

Nitz, Hermann. Die Materialen für Buch und Bucheinband. 3d ed. Halle, Knapp, 1953. 156p.

Nixon, Howard M. Broxbourne Library. Styles and designs of bookbinding from the twelfth to the twentieth century. London, Maggs Bros., 1956. 250p.

_____. English Restoration bookbindings: Samuel Mearne and his con- temporaries. London, British Museum, 1974. 48p.

_____. Five centuries of English bookbinding. London, Scolar Press, 1978. 232p.

Nordlunde, C. Volmer. Thomas James Cobden-Sanderson, bogbinder og bog- trykker. Copenhagen, Busck, 1957. 79p.

Oldham, James B. Blind panels of English binders. Cambridge, Univ. Press, 1958. 55p.

_____. English blind-stamp bindings. Cambridge, Univ. Press, 1952. 72p.

Pierpont Morgan Library, N.Y. Sixteenth century gold-tooled bookbindings in the Pierpont Morgan Library. By Howard M. Nixon. N.Y., 1971. 263p.

Park, Henrik. Modern Danish bindings. Copenhagen, Anker Kysters, 1950. 31p.

Prideaux, Sarah T. Bookbinders and their craft. London, Zaehnsdorf, 1903. 298p.

Ramsden, Charles. Bookbinders of the United Kingdom (outside London) 1780-1830. London, 1954. 250p.

_____. French bookbinders 1789-1848. London, Humphries, 1950. 228p.

_____. London bookbinders 1780-1840. London, Batsford, 1956. 155p.

Robinson, Ivor. Introducing bookbinding. London, Batsford, 1968. 112p.

Roquet, Antoine E. Les reliures français (1500-1800). Paris, Paul,
    Huard and Guillemin, 1893. 416p.

Rosner, Charles. The growth of the book jacket. Cambridge, Harvard
    Univ. Press, 1954. 74p.

Rudbeck, Gustaf. Broderade bokband fraan aeldre tid i svenska samlinger.
    Stockholm, 1925. 110p.

_____. Svenska bokband under nyare bidrag till svensk bokbinderhis-
    toria. Stockholm, 1912-14. 3 vols. in 2.

Sadleir, Michael. The evolution of publishers' binding styles 1770-1900.
    London, Constable, 1930. 96p.

_____. XIX century fiction: a bibliographical record. London,
    Constable, 1951. 2 vols.

Samford, C. Clement and Hemphill, John M. Bookbinding in colonial
    Virginia. Charlottesville, Univ. Press of Virginia, 1966. 185p.

Sarre, Friedrich P. Islamic bookbindings. London, Paul, Trench, Trübner,
    1923. 167p.

Schauer, Georg K. Deutsche Buchkunst 1890 bis 1960. Hamburg,
    Maximilian-Gesellschaft, 1963. 2 vols.

Schjoldager, Astrid. Bokbind og bokbindere i Norge inntil 1850. Oslo,
    1927. 348p.

Schrieber, Heinrich. Jakob Krause. Stuttgart, Hettler, 1953. 79p.

_____. Studien zum Bilderschmuck der deutschen Renaissance-Einbände.
    Wiesbaden, Harrassowitz, 1959. 151p.

Schunke, Ilse, ed. Beiträge zum Rollen- und Platteneinband im 16.
    Jahrhundert. K. Haebler zum 80 Geburtstage...gewidmet. Leipzig,
    Harrassowitz, 1937. 408p.

Smith, Philip. New directions in bookbinding. Cincinnati, Von Nostrand
    Reinhold, 1975. 208p.

Société de la Reliure Originale. Exposition...accompagnée d'une présen-
    tation de reliures ayant appartenu à Jean Grolier. Paris, 1959.
    150p.

Steenbock, Frauke. Der kirchliche Prachteinband in frühen Mittelalter
    von den Anfängen bis zum der Beginn der Gotik.   Berlin, Deutsche
    Verlag für Kunstwissenschaft, 1965. 237p.

Sterne, Harold E. Catalogue of nineteenth century bindery equipment.
    Cincinnati, Ye Olde Printery, 1979. 271p. illus.

Strachan, Walter J. The artist and the book in France; the 20th century
    livre d'artiste. London, Peter Owen, 1969. 368p.

Tauber, Maurice F., ed. Library binding manual; a handbook of useful
    procedures for the maintenance of library volumes. Boston,
    Library Binding Institute, 1972. 185p.

Taylor, John R. The art nouveau book in Britain. Edinburgh, Paul
    Harris, 1979. 175p.

Thomas, Henry. Early Spanish bookbindings xi-xv centuries. Oxford,
    Printed for the Bibliographical Society at the Univ. Press, Oxford,
    1939 (for 1936). 65p.

Thompson, Lawrence S. Books in our time. Wash., D.C., Consortium Press,
    1972. 356p.

Toldo, Vittorio de. L'arte italiana della legature del libro. Milan,
    1923. 29p.

Uzanne, Octave. The French bookbinders of the eighteenth century.
    Chicago, Caxton Club, 1904. 133p.

_____. La reliure moderne artistique et fantaisiste. Paris, Rouveyre,
    1887. 263p.

Valéry, Paul et al. Paul Bonet. Paris, Blaizot, 1945. 259p.

Vatican. Biblioteca Vaticana. Legatura papali da Eugenio IV a Paolo VI.
    Vatican City, 1977. 168p.

Vico, Arnaldo dei. L'arte nella legature moderne, i legatore e il libro.
    Rome, 1931. 109p.

Wakeman, Geoffrey. English marbled papers; a documentary history.
    Loughborough, Plough Press, 1980? 27p.

Weber, Carl J. Fore-edge painting; an historical survey of a curious
    art in book decoration. Irvington-on-Husdon, N.Y., Harvey House,
    1966. 223p.

_____. A thousand and one fore-edge paintings. Waterville, Me.,
    Colby College Press, 1949. 194p.

Wiberg, Carl G. Sveriges bokbinderidkareforening, 75 ar. Stockholm,
    Sveriges Bokbinderidkareforening, 1975. 165p.

Zaehnsdorf, Joseph. The art of bookbinding. London, Bell, 1879. 187p.

CHECKLIST OF TITLES
FOR A COLLEGE LIBRARY

Allen, Sue. Victorian bookbindings; a pictorial survey. rev. ed.
Chicago, Univ. of Chicago Press, 1976. 53p. 3 microfiche sheets
in pocket.

Arnold, Thomas W. and Grohmann, Adolph. The Islamic book. N.Y.,
Harcourt, Brace, 1929. 130p.

The arts of the book in central Asia, 14th-16th centuries. Oleg
Akimushkin et al. General editor, Basil Gray. Paris, UNESCO, 1979.
314p.

Banister, Manly M. Bookbinding as a handcraft. N.Y., Sterling, 1975.
160p.

Béraldi, Henri. La reliure du xixe siècle. Paris, Conquet, 1895-1897.
4 vols.

Bibliotheca Corviniana; the library of King Matthias of Hungary. Shannon,
Irish Univ. Press, 1969. 398p.

Bodleian Library. Fine bindings 1500-1700 from Oxford libraries;
catalogue of an exhibition. Oxford, 1968. 144p.

_____. Gold-tooled bookbindings. Oxford, 1951. 7p. 24 plates.

_____. Textile and embroidered bindings. Oxford, 1971. 30p.

British Museum. Bookbindings from the library of Jean Grolier; a loan
exhibition 23 Sept.-31 Oct. 1965. London, 1965. 75p.

Burdett, Eric. The craft of bookbinding. Newton Abbot, David and
Charles, 1975. 400p.

Carter, John. Binding variants in English publishing 1820-1900. London,
Constable, 1932. 172p.

_____. More binding variants. London, Constable, 1938. 52p.

_____. Publisher's cloth; an outline history of publisher's binding
in England 1820-1900. N.Y., Bowker, 1935. 52p.

Clough, Eric A. Bookbinding for librarians. London, Association of
Assistant Librarians, 1957. 204p.

Cockerell, Douglas. Bookbinding and the care of books. 5th ed. London,
Pitman, 1953. 345p.

Comparato, Frank E. Books for the millions. Harrisburg, Stackpole, 1971. 374p.

Craig, Maurice J. Irish bookbindings 1600-1800. London, Cassell, 1954. 47p.

Crauzat, Ernest de. La reliure française de 1900 à 1925. Paris, 1932. 2 vols.

Darley, Lionel S. Introduction to bookbinding. London, Faber and Faber, 1965. 118p.

Davenport, Cyril J. Cameo book-stamps figured and described. London, Edward Arnold, 1911. 207p.

_____. English heraldic book-stamps. London, Constable, 1909. 450p.

Devauchelle, Roger. La reliure en France de ses origines à nos jours. Paris, Rousseau-Girard, 1959-61. 3 vols.

Deville, Etienne. La reliure française. Paris, Van Oest, 1930-31. 2 vols.

Diehl, Edith. Bookbinding, its background and technique. N.Y., Rinehart, 1946. 2 vols.

Early American bookbindings from the collection of Michael Papantonio. N.Y., Pierpont Morgan Library with the American Antiquarian Society, Cornell and Princeton Univ. libraries and the Univ. of Virginia Library, 1972. 89p.

Foot, Mirjam M. The Henry Davis gift: a collection of bindings. Vol. 1: Studies in the history of bookbinding. London, British Library, 1978. 352p.

Fürstenberg, Jean. Le grand siècle en France et ses bibliophiles. Hamburg, Hauswedell, 1972. 160p. and 60 slides of bindings.

Glaister, Geoffrey A. Glaister's glossary of the book. 2d ed., completely revised. Berkeley, Univ. of California Press, 1979. 551p.

Goldschmidt, Ernst P. Gothic and renaissance bookbindings. London, Benn, 1928. 2 vols.

Gruel, Léon. Manuel historique et bibliographique de l'amateur de reliures. Paris, Gruel and Engelmann, 1887-1905. 2 vols.

Haemmerle, Albert and Hirsch, Olga. Buntpapier. 2d ed. Munich, Callwey, 1977. 255p.

Harrod, Leonard M. The librarian's glossary. 4th ed. London, Deutsch, 1977. 903p.

Helwig, Hellmuth. Einbandfälschungen. Stuttgart, Hettler, 1968. 98p.

_____. Handbuch der Einbandkunde. Hamburg, Maximilian-Gesellschaft, 1953-55. 3 vols.

Herbst, Hermann. Bibliographie der Buchbinderei-Literatur. Leipzig,
    Hiersemann, 1933. 169p.

Hobson, Anthony R. Apollo and Pegasus; an inquiry into the formation
    and dispersal of a renaissance library. Amsterdam, Philo Press-
    Van Heusden, 1975. 250p.

Hobson, Geoffrey D. Bindings in Cambridge libraries; seventy-two plates
    with notes. Cambridge, Univ. Press, 1929. 179p.

_____. English binding before 1500. Cambridge, Univ. Press, 1929.
    58p.

_____. Maioli, Canevari and others. London, Benn, 1926. 178p.

_____. Les reliures à la fanfare. 2d ed. Amsterdam, Van Heusden,
    1970. 151, 17p.

Holme, Charles, ed. The art of the book; a review of some recent
    European and American work in typography, page decoration and bind-
    ing. London, Studio, 1914. 276p.

Horne, Herbert P. The binding of books; an essay in the history of gold-
    tooled bindings. London, Paul, Trench, Trübner, 1894. 224p. 2d ed.,
    rev. and corrected, 1915.

Horton, Carolyn. Cleaning and preserving bindings and related materials.
    2d ed. Chicago, American Library Association, 1969. 87p.

Howe, Ellic. A list of London bookbinders 1648-1815. London, Bibliogra-
    phical Society, 1950. 105p.

Hunt Institute for Botanical Documentation. The tradition of fine bind-
    ing in the 20th century. Pittsburg, the Hunt Institute and Davis
    and Warde, 1979. 129p. (exhibit catalog)

Jamieson, Eleanore. English embossed bindings 1825-1850. Cambridge,
    Univ. Press, 1972. 95p.

Jennett, Seán. The making of books. 4th ed. London, Faber and Faber,
    1967. 512p.

Kafka, Francis J. How to clothbind a paperback book; a step-by-step
    guide for beginners. N.Y., Dover, 1980. 24p.

Kyriss, Ernst. Katalog historischer Einbände des 11 bis 20 Jahrhunderts
    aus der Württembergischen Landesbibliothek. Stuttgart, 1955. 48p.

_____. Verzierte gotische Einbände im alten deutschen Sprachgebiet.
    Stuttgart, Hettler, 1951-58. 4 vols.

Lehmann-Haupt, Hellmuth. Bookbinding in America. N.Y., Bowker, 1967.
    293p.

Lexikon des Buchwesens. Hrsg. von Joachim Kirchner. Stuttgart, Hierse-
    mann, 1952-56. 4 vols.

López Serrano, Matilde. La encuadernación española; breve historia.
    Madrid, Asociacion de Bibliotecarios, Archivos y Arquelogos, 1972.
    146p.

Loring, Rosamond. Decorated book papers. 2d ed. Ed. by Philip Hofer.
    Cambridge, Harvard Univ. Press, 1952. 171p.

Loubier, Hans. Der Bucheinband von seinen Anfängen bis zum Ende des 18.
    Jahrhunderts. 2d ed. Leipzig, Klinkhardt and Biermann, 1926. 272p.

Lydenberg, Harry M. and Archer, John. The care and repair of books.
    Rev. by John Alden. N.Y., Bowker, 1960. 122p.

McLean, Ruari. Victorian book design and colour printing. 2d ed.
    London, Faber and Faber, 1972. 241p.

_____. Victorian publishers' bookbindings in cloth and leather.
    London, Gordon Fraser, 1974. 160p.

Mansfield, Edgar. Modern design in bookbinding work. London, Peter
    Owen, 1966. 119p.

Marinis, Tammaro de. La legatura artistica in Italia nei secoli xv e xvi.
    Florence, Fratelli Alinari, Istituto de Edizioni Artistiche, 1960.
    3 vols.

Mejer, Wolfgang. Bibliographie der Buchbinderei-Literatur. Leipzig,
    Hiersemann, 1925. 208p.

Mick, Ernst W. Altes Buntpapiere. Dortmund, Harenberg, 1979. 175p.

Middleton, Bernard C. A history of English craft bookbinding technique.
    N.Y., Hafner, 1963. 307p.

_____. The restoration of leather bindings. Chicago, American
    Library Association, 1972. 201p.

Mitchell, William S. A history of Scottish bookbinding 1432 to 1650.
    Edinburgh, Oliver and Boyd, 1955. 150p.

Morrow, Carolyn C. and Schoenly, Steven B. A conservation bibliography
    for librarians, archivists, and administrators. N.Y., Whitston,
    1979. 271p.

Needham, Paul. Twelve centuries of bookbindings 400-1600. N.Y.,
    Pierpont Morgan Library, Oxford Univ. Press, 1979. 338p.

Nitz, Hermann. Die Materialen für Buch und Bucheinband. 3d ed. Halle,
    Knapp, 1953. 156p.

Nixon, Howard M. Broxbourne Library, Styles and designs of bookbinding
    from the twelfth to the twentieth century. London, Maggs Bros.,
    1956. 250p.

_____. Five centuries of English bookbinding. London, Scolar Press,
    1978. 232p.

Oldham, James B. Blind panels of English binders. Cambridge, Univ.
    Press, 1958. 55p.

_____. English blind-stamp bindings. Cambridge, Univ. Press, 1952.
    72p.

Pierpont Morgan Library, N.Y. 16th century gold-tooled bookbindings in
    the Pierpont Morgan Library. By Howard M. Nixon, N.Y., 1971. 263p.

Prideaux, Sarah T. Bookbinders and their craft. London, Zaehnsdorf,
    1903. 298p.

Ramsden, Charles. Bookbinders of the United Kingdom (outside London)
    1780-1840. London, 1954. 250p.

_____. French bookbinders 1789-1848. London, Humphries, 1950. 228p.

_____. London bookbinders 1780-1840. London, Batsford, 1956. 155p.

Robinson, Ivor. Introducing bookbinding. London, Batsford, 1968. 112p.

Roquet, Antoine E. Les relieurs français (1500-1800). Biographie
    critique et anecdotique...par Ernest Thoinan [pseud.] Paris, Paul,
    Huard and Guillemin, 1893. 416p.

Rosner, Charles. The growth of the book jacket. Cambridge, Harvard
    Univ. Press, 1954. 74p.

Sadleir, Michael. The evolution of publishers' binding styles 1770-1900.
    London, Constable, 1930. 96p.

_____. XIX century fiction; a bibliographical record. London,
    Constable, 1951. 2 vols.

Samford, C. Clement and Hemphill, John M. Bookbinding in colonial
    Virginia. Charlottesville, Univ. Press of Virginia, 1966. 185p.

Sarre, Friedrich P. Islamic bookbindings. London, Paul, Trench, Trübner,
    1923. 167p.

Schauer, Georg K. Deutsche Buchkunst 1890 bis 1960. Hamburg, Maximilian-
    Gesellschaft, 1963. 2 vols.

Schreiber, Heinrich. Studien zum Bilderschmuck der deutschen
    Renaissance-Einbände, Wiesbaden, Harrassowitz, 1959. 151p.

Smith, Philip. New directions in bookbinding. Cincinnati, Van Nostrand
    Reinhold, 1975. 208p.

Steenbock, Frauke. Der kirchliche Prachteinband in frühen Mittelalter
    von den Anfängen bis zum der Beginn der Gotik. Berlin, Deutsche
    Verlag für Kunstwissenschaft, 1965. 237p.

Sterne, Harold E. Catalogue of nineteenth century bindery equipment.
    Cincinnati, Ye Olde Printery, 1979. 271p.

Strachan, Walter J. The artist and the book in France; the 20th century livre d'artiste. London, Peter Owen, 1969. 368p.

Tauber, Maurice F., ed. Library binding manual; a handbook of useful procedures for the maintenance of library volumes. Boston, Library Binding Institute, 1972. 185p.

Taylor, John R. The art nouveau book in Britain. Edinburgh, Paul Harris, 1979. 175p.

Thomas, Henry. Early Spanish bookbindings xi-xv centuries. Oxford, 1939 (for 1936). 65p.

Thompson, Lawrence S. Books in our time. Wash., D.C., Consortium Press, 1972. 356p.

Toldo, Vittorio de. L'arte italiana della legatura del libro. Milan, 1923. 29p.

Uzanne, Octave. The French bookbinders of the eighteenth century. Chicago, Caxton Club, 1904. 133p.

_____. La reliure moderne artistique et fantaisiste. Paris, Rouveyre, 1887. 263p.

Wakeman, Geoffrey. English marbled papers; a documentary history. Loughborough, Plough Press, 1980? 27p.

Weber, Carl J. Fore-edge painting; an historical survey of a curious art in book decoration. Irvington-on-Hudson, N.Y., Harvey House, 1966. 223p.

_____. A thousand and one fore-edge paintings. Waterville, Me., Colby College Press, 1949. 194p.

Young, Laura S. Bookbinding and conservation by hand; a working guide. N.Y., Bowker, 1981. 273p.

CHECKLIST OF TITLES
FOR A MEDIUM-SIZED
PUBLIC LIBRARY

Allen, Sue. Victorian bookbindings; a pictorial survey. rev. ed. Chicago, Univ. of Chicago Press, 1976. 53p. 3 microfiche sheets in pocket.

Arnold, Thomas W. and Grohmann, Adolph. The Islamic book. N.Y., Harcourt, Brace, 1929. 130p.

Banister, Manly M. Bookbinding as a handcraft. N.Y., Sterling, 1975. 160p.

Bodleian Library. Gold-tooled bookbindings. Oxford, 1951. 7p. 24 plates.

_____. Textile and embroidered bindings. Oxford, 1971. 30p.

Carter, John. Publisher's cloth; an outline history of publisher's binding in England 1820-1900. N.Y., Bowker, 1935. 52p.

Clough, Eric A. Bookbinding for librarians. London, Association of Assistant Librarians, 1957. 204p.

Cockerell, Douglas. Bookbinding and the care of books. 5th ed. London, Pitman, 1953. 345p.

Comparato, Frank E. Books for the millions. Harrisburg, Stackpole, 1971. 374p.

Darley, Lionel S. Introduction to bookbinding. London, Faber and Faber, 1965. 118p.

Davenport, Cyril J. Cameo book-stamps figured and described. London, Edward Arnold, 1911. 207p.

_____. English heraldic book-stamps. London, Constable, 1909. 450p.

Deville, Etienne. La reliure française. Paris, Van Oest, 1930-31. 2 vols.

Diehl, Edith. Bookbinding, its background and technique. N.Y., Rinehart, 1946. 2 vols.

Early American bookbindings from the collection of Michael Papantonio. N.Y., Pierpont Morgan Library with the American Antiquarian Society, Cornell and Princeton Univ. libraries and the Univ. of Virginia Library, 1972. 89p.

Fürstenberg, Jean. Le grand siècle en France et ses bibliophiles.
Hamburg, Hauswedell, 1972. 160p. and 60 slides of bindings.

Glaister, Geoffrey A. Glaister's glossary of the book. 2d ed.,
completely revised. Berkeley, Univ. of California Press, 1979.
551p.

Goldschmidt, Ernst P. Gothic and Renaissance bookbindings. London,
Benn, 1928. 2 vols.

Gruel, Léon. Manuel historique et bibliographique de l'amateur de
reliures. Paris, Gruel and Engelmann, 1887-1905. 2 vols.

Haemmerle, Albert and Hirsch, Olga. Buntpapier. 2d ed. Munich,
Callwey, 1977. 255p.

Harrod, Leonard M. The librarians' glossary. 4th rev. ed. London,
Deutsch, 1977. 903p.

Helwig, Hellmuth. Einbandfälschungen. Stuttgart, Hettler, 1968. 98p.

_____. Handbuch der Einbandkunde. Hamburg, Maximilian-Gesellschaft,
1953-55. 3 vols.

Hetzer, Linda. Traditional crafts. Milwaukee, Raintree, 1978. 48p.
(juvenile)

Hobson, Geoffrey D. English binding before 1500. Cambridge, Univ.
Press, 1929. 58p.

_____. Apollo and Pegasus; an inquiry into the formation and dis-
persal of a renaissance library. Amsterdam, Philo Press-Van Heusden,
1975. 250p.

Horton, Carolyn. Cleaning and preserving bindings and related materials.
2d ed. Chicago, American Library Association, 1969. 87p.

Howe, Ellic. A list of London bookbinders 1648-1815. London, Bibliographical Society, 1950. 105p.

Hunt Institute for Botanical Documentation. The tradition of fine bookbinding in the 20th century. Pittsburgh, the Hunt Institute and
Davis and Warde, 1979. 129p. (exhibit catalog)

Indiana University. Lilly Library. British bookbinding today. With an
introduction by Edgar Mansfield. Bloomington, 1976. 65p.

Jennett, Seán. The making of books. 4th ed. London, Faber and Faber,
1967. 512p.

Kafka, Francis J. How to clothbind a paperback book; a step-by-step
guide for beginners. N.Y., Dover, 1980. 24p.

Kyriss, Ernst. Katalog historischer Einbände des 11 bis 20 Jahrhunderts
aus der Württembergischen Landesbibliothek. Stuttgart, 1955. 48p.

Lehmann-Haupt, Hellmuth. Bookbinding in America. N.Y., Bowker, 1967.
     293p.

Lexikon des Buchwesens. Hrsg. von Joachim Kirchner. Stuttgart,
     Hiersemann, 1952-56. 4 vols.

López Serrano, Matilde. La encuadernación española; breve historia.
     Madrid, Asociacion de Bibliotecarios, Archivos y Arquelogos, 1972.
     146p.

Loring, Rosamond. Decorated book papers. 2d ed. Ed. by Philip Hofer.
     Cambridge, Harvard Univ. Press, 1952. 171p.

Lydenberg, Harry M. and Archer, John. The care and repair of books.
     Rev. by John Alden. N.Y., Bowker, 1960. 122p.

McLean, Ruari. Victorian book design and colour printing. 2d ed.
     London, Faber and Faber, 1972. 241p.

_____. Victorian publishers' bookbindings in cloth and leather.
     London, Gordon Fraser, 1974. 160p.

Mansfield, Edgar. Modern design in bookbinding work. London, Peter Owen,
     1966. 119p.

Marinis, Tammaro de. La legatura artistica in Italia nei secoli xv e xvi.
     Florence, Fratelli Alinari, Istituto di Edizioni Artistiche, 1960.
     3 vols.

Middleton, Bernard C. A history of English craft bookbinding technique.
     N.Y., Hafner, 1963. 307p.

_____. The restoration of leather bindings. Chicago, American
     Library Association, 1972. 201p.

Morrow, Carolyn C. and Schoenly, Steven B. A conservation bibliography
     for librarians, archivists, and administrators. N.Y., Whitston,
     1979. 271p.

Needham, Paul. Twelve centuries of bookbindings 400-1600. N.Y.,
     Pierpont Morgan Library, Oxford Univ. Press, 1979. 338p.

Nixon, Howard M. Broxbourne Library. Styles and designs of bookbinding
     from the twelfth to the twentieth century. London, Maggs Bros.,
     1956. 250p.

_____. Five centuries of English bookbinding. London, Scolar Press,
     1978. 232p.

Purdy, Susan. Books for you to make. Philadelphia, Lippincott, 1973.
     96p. (juvenile)

Ramsden, Charles. Bookbinders of the United Kingdom (outside London)
     1780-1840. London, 1954. 250p.

_____. French bookbinders 1789-1848. London, Humphries, 1950. 228p.

Ramsden, Charles. London bookbinders 1780-1840. London, Batsford, 1956. 155p.

Robinson, Ivor. Introducing bookbinding. London, Batsford, 1968. 112p.

Rosner, Charles. The growth of the book jacket. Cambridge, Harvard Univ. Press, 1954. 74p.

Sadleir, Michael. The evolution of publishers' binding styles 1770-1900. London, Constable, 1930. 96p.

_____. XIX century fiction: a bibliographical record. London, Constable, 1951. 2 vols.

Samford, C. Clement and Hemphill, John M. Bookbinding in colonial Virginia. Charlottesville, Univ. Press of Virginia, 1966. 185p.

Smith, Philip. New directions in bookbinding. Cincinnati, Van Nostrand Reinhold, 1975. 208p.

Sterne, Harold E. Catalogue of nineteenth century bindery equipment. Cincinnati, Ye Olde Printery, 1979. 271p.

Strachan, Walter J. The artist and the book in France; the 20th century livre d'artiste. London, Peter Owen, 1969. 368p.

Tauber, Maurice F., ed. Library binding manual; a handbook of useful procedures for the maintenance of library volumes. Boston, Library Binding Institute, 1972. 185p.

Taylor, John R. The art nouveau book in Britain. Edinburgh, Paul Harris, 1979. 175p.

Thompson, Lawrence S. Books in our time. Wash., D.C., Consortium Press, 1972. 356p.

Weber, Carl J. Fore-edge painting; an historical survey of a curious art in book decoration. Irvington-on-Hudson, N.Y., Harvey House, 1966. 223p.

_____. A thousand and one fore-edge paintings. Waterville, Me., Colby College Press, 1949. 194p.

Weiss, Harvey. How to make your own books. N.Y., Crowell, 1974. 71p. (juvenile)

Young, Laura S. Bookbinding and conservation by hand; a working guide. N.Y., Bowker, 1981. 273p.

LIST OF BINDERS,
BINDING DESIGNERS,
AND BINDING DECORATORS

Adam, Paul (1849-1931), German binder

Adams, Katherine (1862- ?), British binder

Adams, Ralph Randolph, 19th century American binder

Adenis, Georges, 20th century French binding decorator

Adler, Rose (1890-1959), 20th century French master binder

Aitken, Robert, early American binder in Philadelphia

Alegria, José, 19th century Spanish binder

Amand, Pierre (Chevannes dit), 19th century French binder

Ameline, Paul, 20th century French binder

Andersson, Nils Bernhard, 19-20th century Swedish binder

Andrus, Silas, 19th century American binder

Antoine-Legrain, Jacques (1907-   ), French binder

Antona, Jacqueline, 20th century French binding designer

Apiarius, early Swiss binder

Armstrong, Margaret N. (1867-1944), American binder

Baden, Jakob (1861-1940), Danish binder

Badier, Florimond, 17th century French binder

Baer, George, 20th century American binder

Bagguley, G. T., 19th century English binder

Baldensheym, Adolar, 16th century German binder

Barclay, Andrew (1738-1823), Scottish binder of Boston

Barkell, William, 20th century Swedish binder

Bartlett, Roger (1633-1712), English binder

Baumgarten, John, 18th century German binder in London

Bauzonnet, Antoine (1795- ?), 19th century French binder

Beardsley, Aubrey (1872-1898), English artist, illustrator, and decorator
   of bindings

Beck, Franz (1814-1888), German binder in Stockholm

Bedford, Francis (1799-1883), English binder

Behrens, Peter (1868-1940), German painter, architect, and designer of
   bindings

Belville, Eugène, 19-20th century French binder

Benedict, Vida G., 20th century American binder

Benedict family, 19th century binders in London

Berg, Jörgen, 20th century Danish binder

Berggren, Johan, 18th century Swedish binder in Lund

Bernard, Marguerite, 20th century French binder

Bertheley, Thomas, 16th century English binder

Bertin, Theodore Pierre (fl. 1800-1818), Paris binder

Billow, Anders, 20th century Swedish binding designer

Billow, Eva, 20th century Swedish binding designer

Bindesbøll, Thorvald (1846-1908), Danish architect, ceramist, painter,
   and designer of bindings

Bleyl, Werner (1918-   ), German binder

Bohn, John (1757-1843), German binder in London

Bonet, Paul (1889-1971), Belgian binder in France

Bonfils, Robert (1886-1972), painter, engraver, illustrator, and
   decorator of bindings

Bonnor, William, 18th century English binder

Bonsal, Louis, 19th century Maryland binder

Boppenhausen family, 18th century Danish binders

Borsdamm, John H., 20th century German binder in the United States

Boyer (or Boyet), French family of printers, 1670-1730

Bozérian brothers, 19th century French binders

Bradel, Alexis-Pierre, 18th century Paris binder

Bradel, Pierre-Jean, 19th century French binder

Bradford, William (1663-1752), American printer and binder

Bradley, Abraham, 18th century Irish binder

Bradley, William H. (1868-1962), American typographer, illustrator,
    designer of bindings

Brech, Preben (1931-   ), Danish binder

Brindley, John, 18th century English binder

Brockman, James R. (1946-   ), English binder

Brown, Alexander (1766-1848), Scottish bookseller

Brugalla, Emilio (1901-   ), Spanish binder

Brugalla, Santiago (1929-   ), Spanish binder

Buglass, Caleb (died 1797), American binder in Phila.

Bulkley, M. E. (Miss), 19th century American binder

Cains, Anthony, 20th century English binder in Ireland

Calkin, P., 19th century English binder

Canapé, Georges (died 1937), Paris binder

Canapé, J., 19-20th century French binder

Capé, 19th century Paris binder

Carsi y Vidal, Pascual, 19th century Spanish binder in Madrid

Caumont, Auguste Marie de, (Comte) (1743-1833), a French nobleman who con-
    ducted a binding workshop in London between 1796 and 1814

Caxton, William, 15th century English printer and binder

Chambolle, 19th century French binder. His son, R. Chambolle (died
    1915), was also a binder.

Champs (died 1912), 19th century French binder

Chapin, Elizabeth G., 19th century American binder

Chapman, Christopher, 18th century English binder

Charrière, Gérard (1935-   ), Swiss binder in the United States

Chivers, Cedric, 19th century English binder

Claessens, Paul, 19th century Belgian binder

Clarke, John (fl. 1825-56), English binder

Clément, Daniel L. (1820-1877), Danish binder

Clements, Jeff (1934-   ), English binder

Cobden-Sanderson, Thomas J. (1840-1922), English typographer and binder

Cockerell, Douglas, 20th century English binder

Cockerell, Sydney M., 20th century English binder

Coghlan, James P., 18th century printer, publisher, and binder in London

Cohen, Lion (c1756-1802), Jewish binder in the Hague

Coloander, Johan K. (fl. 1796), Swedish binder

Colombo, Pio, 20th century Italian binder

Contreras, Abraham, 20th century Chilean binder

Corfmat family, 19th century French binders

Coronensis, Lucas, 15th century Hungarian binder

Coster, Germaine de, 20th century French binding designer

Courteval (fl. 1796-1836), French binder

Coverley, Roger de (1831- ?), English binder in London

Crane, Walter (1845-1915), English painter, illustrator, and binding
    designer

Cretté, Georges (1893-   ), Paris binder

Creuzevault, Henri (1905-   ), French master binder

Cross, Austin J., 19-20th century Australian binder in the United States

Currie, C. B. (Miss) (died about 1940), English(?) painter of miniatures
    on ivory on Cosway bindings

Cuzin, Francisque (1836-1891), Paris binder and gilder

Czeschka, Carl Otto (1878-1960), Austrian painter, architect, and
    designer of bindings

Damiano da Moile (alias de Bochalariis), 15th century Italian binder

David, Salomon (died 1920), French binder

Davies, William, 18th century binder in Phila.

Dawson, Thomas, 18th century Cambridge binder

Day, Lewis F. (1845-1910), designer of textiles, tiles, glass, and book-bindings. A decorative artist and writer on ornament

Dean, Christopher, 19th century designer in Glasgow and London

Deforge, Isidore, 19th century French binder

Denck, G. Hermann, 19th century German binder

Denslow, William W. (1856-1915), American painter, illustrator, and binding designer

Derôme family, 17-19th century French binders. The most famous was Nicolas Derôme le Jeune (1731-1788). Jacques-Antoine Derôme (1698-1760) was a French master binder and gilder.

Despierres, 19th century French binder (preferred printer of Napoleon III)

Devauchelle, Roger, 20th century French binder

Diehl, Edith (died 1953), 20th century American binder and author

Dorfner, Otto (1885-1955), 20th century German binder

Douceur, Louis, 18th century French binder

Dubuisson, Pierre-Paul (1707-1762), 18th century French heraldic designer and gilder. Binder to Louis XV in 1758.

Dudley, Fanny, 20th century American binder

Dudley, Robert (fl. 1858-91), English designer of bindings

Duffel, Wouter van, 13th century Belgian binder

Dumas, Hélène, 20th century French binder

Dunand, Jean (1877-1942), Swiss sculptor and dinandier in France. Famous for his lacquer bindings.

Duplanil. Distinguished family of binders in 19th century Paris

Duru, Hippolyte (died 1884), French binder

Dusel, Philip (1955-   ), American binder

Duseuil (also Dusseuil, Du Seuil, or De Seuil) (1673-1746), French binder

Eberhardt, Fritz (1917-   ), Silesian binder and calligrapher in Phila.

Eberhardt, Fritz (Mrs.), 20th century binder and calligrapher in Phila.

Eckmann, Otto (1865-1902), German painter, illustrator, decorator, and designer of bindings and book jackets

Edwards family, 18th century binders in Halifax and London.   James Edwards specialized in binding in transparent vellum.

Elliott, Thomas (fl. 1703-1762/63), English binder

Endter, Georg, 16th century German binder

Engelmann, Edmond, 19th century binder in France

Eschmann, Jean (1896-   ), Swiss binder in the United States

Etherington, Don (1935-   ), English binder in the United States

Evans, Henry (fl. 1650-1676), English binder

Eve, Clovis (fl. 1584-1634), French binder

Eve, Nicholas, 16th century French binder

Evetts, Deborah, 20th century English binder in the United States

Fahey, Herbert, 20th century American binder

Fahey, Peter, 20th century American binder

Fairbrother, Samuel (fl. 1723-49), binder in Ireland

Falkner, George, 19th century Manchester binder

Fazakerley, John (fl. 1877-1891), binder in Liverpool

Fazakerley, Thomas, 19th century binder in Liverpool

Fenden, Martinus V. (died 1742), Polish binder in Denmark

Ferrini, Agnolo (fl. 1473-1488), 15th century Italian binder

Field, John M. (1939-   ), American binder

Fischer, Janos, 19th century Hungarian binder

Fisher, George (1879-1970), English printer and binder

Flötner, Peter (c.1485-1546), German binding decorator

Flyge, J. L., 19th century Danish binder

Fogel, Johannes, 15th century German binder

Foote, Florence, 19th century American binder

Franck, Peter, 20th century German binder in the United States

Franzese, Niccolò, 16th century Italian binder

Frost, Gary L. (1941–   ), American binder

Galván, José, 20th century Spanish binder. His two sons, José and
    Antonio, are also binders.

Ganiaris, Andreas (1926–   ), Greek binder

Gardner, Anthony (1886-1973), English binder

Gavere, Antoine de, 15th century Belgian binder

Gérard, Liliane (1946–   ), Belgian binder

Gerlach, Gerhard, 20th century German binder in the United States

Gerlach, Kathryn, 20th century binder in the United States

Germain, L. D. (Mme), 20th century French binder

Giannini, Giulio Guido (1877– ?), 20th century Italian binder

Ginain, 19th century French binder in Paris

Giraldon, Ferdinand, 20th century French binding designer

Glaister, Donald W. (1945–   ), American binder

Gomez, Gabriel, 18th century Spanish binder

Gonet, Jean de, 20th century French binder

Goodwin, James, 18th century American binder

Gosden, Thomas, 19th century English binder

Gozzi, Dante, 17th century Italian binder

Gozzi, Pietro (1934–   ), Italian binder

Gozzi, Rolando, 17th century Italian binder

Grabau, John F. (died 1948), American binder

Gras, Madeleine (1891-1958), French binder

Greenhill, Elizabeth (1907–   ), French binder in England

Gruel, Léon (1841-1923), French binder

Gruel, Pierre-Paul (fl.1832-48), French binder

Gruel (Madame), 19th century French binder

Günther, Albert, 20th century Austrian binder

Guillery, Marcontonio, 16th century Italian bookseller and binder

Haas, Renée, 20th century French painter and binding designer

Hagen, Francis van, 17th century Scottish binder

Hardy, C., 19th century French binder

Hardy, Henri, 19-20th century French binder in France and the United
    States

Hayday, James (1796-1872), English binder

Hedberg, Arvid (1872-1949), Swedish binder

Hedberg, Gustaf (1859-1920), Swedish binder

Hedlung, Per, 20th century Swedish binding designer

Heim, Edwin (1945-   ), Swiss master binder

Helmuth, August H. (1714-1777), 18th century Danish binder

Hering, Charles (fl. 1794-1815), German binder in London. Other members
    of the family followed him in the bookbinding business.

Herrera, José Ramón, 18th century binder

Herrick, Gale (1909-   ), American binder

Hertzberg, Edward, 20th century binder in Chicago

Hertzberg, Ernst, 19-20th century binder in Chicago

Hetzel, Pierre-Jules (1814-1886), Paris editor, publisher, and binding
    designer

Hiller, Barbara F. (1927-   ), American binder

Hiort, Niels, 18th century Danish binder

Hofer, Anton, 20th century Austrian binder

Hoffmann, Josef (1870-1956), Austrian architect and designer of bindings

Hofman, P. A. H., 20th century Dutch binder

Holl, John, 18th century English binder in Worcester

Holmboe, Thorolf (1866-1935), Norwegian painter, illustrator, and binding decorator

Holmes, Thomas J., 20th century English binder and gilder in the United States

Horstschulze, Mary (1945-   ), master binder in Germany

Housman, Laurence (1865-1959), English dramatist, essayist, fiction writer, and designer of bindings

Hubbard, Elbert (1856-1915), American author, printer, and book designer. Founder of the Roycroft Press.

Hübel, C. Friedrich, 19th century German binder

Humphreys, Henry N., 19th century English author, illustrator, and designer of bindings

Hutchinson, Hugh, 17th century English binder

Hutchinson, Wesley, 20th century American binder

Image, Selwyn (1849-1930), English painter, illustrator, and designer of bindings

Jacobsen, Oscar, 20th century Danish binder

Jaegle, Martin (1931-   ), Swiss master binder

Jaffé, Meir, 15th century Jewish master binder and copyist

Jahoda, Robert, 20th century Austrian binder

James, Angela (1948-   ), English binder

Johnson, Arthur W. (1920-   ), English binder in London

Joly, 19th century French gilder

Joly fils, 20th century French binder

Jones, Owen (1809-1874), English architect and designer of ornaments and bindings

Jones, Trevor (1931-   ), English binder

Judet, Pascale (1946-   ), French binder in the United States

Kahle, Anne C. (1938–   ), English binder in the United States

Kalthoeber, Christian Samuel (fl. 1790–1825), German binder in England

Kandinsky, Wassily (1866–1944), Russian painter, graphic artist, poet, and designer of covers and jackets for catalogs, art books, and almanacs

Kathedrālis, Mátyás, 15th century Hungarian calligrapher, miniature painter, and designer of bindings

Kersten, Paul (1865–1943), German binder and gilder

Kieffer, René, 19–20th century French binder

Kierger, Kurt, 20th century crafts director of the Gunther bindery in Vienna

Kiessig, Werner (1924–   ), German binder in Berlin

Kinder, Louis H. (1866–1938), German binder in the United States

King, Jessie M. (1876–1948), Scottish illustrator and designer of bindings

King, Nicholas, 18th century Irish binder

Kitcat, George (1774–1821), English binder

Kitcat, James, 19th century English binder

Klos, Abraham van der (1698–c1772), Dutch binder

Knoll, Jean, 20th century French binder

Kohn, Madeleine (1892–1940), English binder in London and Paris

Kraer, Valentin, 18th century binder in Lausanne

Kranz, Frederick, 20th century leatherworker. Worked on hand-tooled leather bindings for the Roycroft Press.

Krause, Jakob (1531–1586), German binder in Augsburg and Dresden

Kretz, Emil, 20th century Swiss binder

Kulche, August (1924–   ), Dutch binder in Belgium

Kumlien, Akke (1884–1949), Swedish calligrapher, type designer, and binder

Kumlien, Bertil, 20th century Swedish binding designer

Kurz, Gotthilf (1923–   ), German master binder

Kyster, Anker (1864–1939), Danish binder

Lahey, Marguerite Duprez (1890-1952), American binder

Lane, Marian U. M., 20th century English binder in the United States

Langrand, Jeanne, 20th century French binder

Lanoë, Charles (1881-1959), French binder

Larrivière, J. N., 19th century French binder in Paris and Lille

Larsen, Knud E., 20th century Danish binder

Latour, Alfred (1888-1964), French painter, engraver, and binding
    designer

Launder, Alfred (1860-1952), English binder in New York City

Launder, William, 19th century English binder in the United States

Lecky, Margaret (1907-   ), American binder

Ledoux, F. R., 19th century French binder in Paris

Le Gascon (fl.1620-1650), Paris binder

Legge, Henry B., 19th century American binder

Legrain, Pierre (1888-1929), French binder

Lehmann, Karl Ernst (1806-1848), Berlin binder

Leighton, Archibald (1742-1799), Scottish binder in London

Leighton, Archibald (1784-1841), Scottish binder who pioneered the use
    of book cloth in the late 1820s

Leighton, John (1822-1912), English designer of bindings and writer

Leland, Charles G. (Hans Breitman, pseud.) (1824-1903), American author
    and binder.

Leman, Hans, Swiss Renaissance binder

Lenoir, 19th century binders in Lyons

Leonard, Christine (1949-   ), Belgian binder

Léotard, Geneviève de, 20th century French binder

Leprêtre, Julian, 20th century binder in Argentina

Lerche, Hans C., (1807-1876), Danish binder

Leroux, Alice, 20th century French binder

Leroux, Georges, 20th century French binder

Lesne, Marthurin-Marie (died 1841), French binder

Lewis, Charles (1786-1836), English binder

Liebe, Georg J., 18th century Danish binder

Linde, Andreas, 18th century German binder in London

Linde, Nils, 20th century Swedish binder

Lindgren, Jorgen L., 20th century Swedish binding designer

Lobisch, Mechthild (1940-   ), German master binder

Lobstein, Alain (1927-   ), French binder

Londenberg, Kurt (1914-   ), German binder

Loring, Rosamond B., 20th century American binder

Lortic (fl.1860-1888), French binder

Lubett, Denise (1922-   ), French binder in London and Paris

Luigi, Maestro, 16th century Italian binder

Lundberg, Ole (1934-   ), Danish master binder

Lundbye, 19th century Danish binding designer

Lunow, Robert, 20th century German gilder and binder in the United States

Lupot(t)i, Bartolomeo di, 15th century Italian binder and miniature
    painter

Lyman, Peter (1695-1768), Danish binder

MacColl, Elizabeth M. (1863-1951), Scottish binder

McCully, Madeleine (1944-   ), Irish binder

MacDonald, James, 19th century Scottish binder in the United States

MacKenzie, John, 19th century London binder

McKenzie, William (died 1817), Irish binder

McLeish, Charles (1859-1949), Scottish binder. His son Charles (1886-   )
    worked with him.

MacLeod, Norman, 19th century Irish binder

Maggs, Bryan D. (1936-   ), English binder

Magnier, Charles, 19th century French binder

Magnin, Lucien (1849-1903), French binder in Lyons

Magnus, Albert (fl.1669-1686), Amsterdam binder

Maillard, Leon, 19-20th century French master of gold tooling

Mairet, François-Ambroise (1786- ?), French binder in Dijon

Mansfield, Edgar, 20th century English and New Zealand binder

Manso, Marino de, 15th century Italian binder in Naples

Martin, Camille (1861-1898), 19th century French painter and decorator
    of bindings in Nancy

Martin, Gabriel Gomez, 18th century Spanish binder

Martin, Pierre-Lucien, 20th century French binder

Martín, Santiago (1775-1828), Spanish binder

Mason, John (1901-   ), English binder

Matthewman, John, 18th century London binder

Matthews, William (1822-1896), Scottish binder in the United States

Matthews, William F. (1898-1977), English binder

Mathieu, Monique, 20th century French binder

Maylander, Emile (1867-1959), French gilder

Mechler, Josias, 16th century Swiss binder in Basel

Mennil, 19th century French binder

Mercer, Daniel, 20th century French binder

Mercher, Henri (1912-   ), French binder

Mercier, Emile, 20th century French binder and gilder

Mercier, Georges, 19th century French binder (probably died before 1920)

Meunier, Charles, 19-20th century French binder and gilder

Meuser, Caspar (died 1593?), German binder

Michel, Marius (or Marius-Michel, Henri F.) (1846-1925), Paris binder

Micke, Christian (1714-1793), Dutch binder

Middlethun, Gregorius, 19th century Norwegian binder

Middleton, Bernard C. (1924–   ), English binder

Miquet, Jean-Paul, 20th century French binder

Milano, Amadio di, 15th century Italian decorator of bindings

Miller, Rachel McMasters, 20th century American binder

Minsky, Richard, 20th century English binder

Moncey, Thérèse, 20th century French binder

Mondange, Raymond, 20th century French gilder

Monnier, Jean Charles (fl.1757–1780), French binder

Monnier, Louis F. (fl.1737–76), French binder

Montagu, Richard (fl.1743–1758), London binder

Moore, Thomas Sturge (1870–1944), English engraver for covers of books
    by W. B. Yeats

Mörck, Niels H., 20th century Swedish binding designer

Morris, Talwin (1865–1911), English industrial designer and designer
    of bindings

Morssing, Greta, 20th century Swedish binder

Mounteney, Leonard (1891–   ), English binder in Chicago

Mozart, Johann G., 18th century German binder (grandfather of the
    composer)

Muller, Markus (1952–   ), Swiss master binder

Mullen, George, 19th century Irish binder

Munch, Ruth (1939–   ), Swiss binder

Munthe, Gerhard P. (1849–1929), Norwegian landscape painter, art writer,
    and decorator of bindings

Nicholson, James B. (died 1901), American binder

Niédrée, C. (1803–1856), German binder in France

Noël, 19th century French binder in Besancon

Nordhoff, Evelyn, 20th century American binder

Noulhac, Henri (1866–1931), French binder

Novoa, Tomas, 18th century Spanish binder

O'Connor, Gemma (1940-   ), Irish binder

Olesen, Erik P. G. (1920-   ), Danish binder

Olesen, Ole (1932-   ), Danish master binder

Os, Thomas van, 18th century Dutch binder

Ouvrard, Pierre (1929-   ), Canadian binder

Padeloup, Antoine-Michel (1685-1758), French binder

Padeloup, Jean, 18th century binder

Pagliarolo, Girolamo (1474- ?), Italian binder

Pagnant (1852-1916), French master binder

Pagnier, Charles, 20th century Paris binder

Parish, Dorothy (1913-   ), American binder

Park, Henrik, 20th century Danish binder

Passaro, Atanasio, 15th century Italian binder

Payne, Roger (1739-1797), English binder

Peche, Dagobert (1887-1923), Austrian painter, architect, and designer
    of bindings

Pechstein, Max (1881-1955), German painter and binding designer of books
    of art scholarship and almanacs

Peller, Hugo, 20th century Swiss binder

Petersen, Heinz, 20th century German binder

Petersen, Immanuel (1836-1903), Danish gilder

Petit, Rémy, 19th century French binder in Paris

Pfaff, Otto, 20th century German binder

Philip, John, 19th century Aberdeen binder

Picques, Claude de, 16th century French binder

Pilon, Gaston, 20th century French binder in the United States

Piper, Jørgen (died 1765), Danish binder

Plantin, Christopher (1520?-1589), Dutch printer, publisher, and binder

Pomeroy, Sandford B., 19-20th century American artist and binding decorator

Powell, Roger, 20th century English binder

Prideaux, Sarah T. (1853-1933), English binder

Press, Alice (1942-   ), American binder

Preston, Emily, 20th century American binder

Purgold, L. G. (died 1830), French binder

Pye, Sybil (1879-1958), English binder

Ranger, Edmund, 17th century American binder in Boston

Raparlier, Paul-Romain (1857-1900), French binder

Rasmussen, Claus, 20th century Danish binder

Ratcliff, John, 17th century English binder in Boston

Ray, Joseph (fl.1705-1718), Irish binder

Refsum, Hans M. (1859-1936), Norwegian binder

Remnant, Frederick (fl.1826), English binder

Remnant, Thomas (fl.1785), English binder

Reussner, Christopher, 17th century Swedish binder

Reynolds, Mary Louise (died 1951), American binder

Rhead, Louis J. (1857-1926), English painter, illustrator, and designer of bindings in the United States

Richenbach, Bernhardin, 15th century German binder

Richenbach, Johannes, 15th century German binder

Ricketts, Charles (1866-1931), English painter, sculptor, wood engraver, writer on art, and designer of bindings

Ritter, Michel (died 1898), French binder

Rivière, Robert (1808-1882), London binder

Robinson, Charles, 19th century English binding designer

Robinson, Ivor (1924-   ), English binder

Roche, Pierre, 19th century French binder

Rochs, 18th century German binder in Potsdam

Roffet, Etienne, 16th century Paris binder

Roffet, Pierre (died 1533), French binder

Rogers, William H. (1825-1873), English designer and illustrator. Designed book covers.

Rohde, Johan, 20th century Danish binder

Roinenen, Juhani (1946-   ), Finnish binder

Rossetti, Dante G. (1828-1882), English poet and binding designer

Roulstone, John (1778-1826), American binder in Boston

Ruban, Pétrus, 19-20th century French binder

Ruette, Antoine (fl.1644-1669), French binder

Ruette, Mace (1584-1644), French binder and bookseller

Rumler, Georg, 16th century German binder

Ruzicka, Joseph and Charles, 19-20th century Czech binders in the United States

Ruzicka, J. Vernon (died 1952), American binder

Ruzicka, Joseph V., Jr., 20th century American binder

Ruzicka, Vaclav, 19th century binder in the United States

Ruzicka (Gross), Marie, 20th century American binder

St. John, Agnes, 20th century American binder

Sancha, Antonio de, 18th century Spanish binder and printer

Sancha, Gabriel de (1746-1820), Spanish binder

Sandgren, August (1893-1934), Danish binder

Sanford, P. B., 20th century American binder in Pittsburgh

Sangorski, Francis (1875-1912), London binder

Sattler, Joseph (1867-1931), German illustrator and designer. Designed bindings.

Saurel, Etienne (c.1714-1784), French binder in The Hague

Sauty, Alfred de (1870-1949), English binder in the United States

Scheer, Bruno (1889-1923?), German master binder

Schmied, François-Louis (1873-1941), Swiss painter, illustrator, master
    engraver, editor, and designer of bindings

Schneidler, Kristoffer (1721-1787), Stockholm binder

Scholl, Sonnfriede (1926-   ), German master binder

Schroeder, Germaine, 20th century French binder

Scott, James (fl.1773-1792), Scottish binder in Edinburgh

Scott, William (fl.1780-1790), Scottish binder

Sears, Mary C. (died 1938), American binder in Boston

Sedgley, Thomas (1684-1761), English binder

Seelig, Juan, 20th century Uruguayan binder

Sellars, David G. (1949-   ), English binder

Shannon, Faith (1938-   ), London binder (born in India)

Simier, René, 19th century Paris binder

Sjöblom, Charles, 20th century Swedish binding designer

Skawonius, Sven E., 20th century Swedish binder

Skinner, Francis, 18th century binder in Newport, R.I.

Skovgaard, Joakin, 20th century Danish binder

Sliegh (or Sleigh), John (fl.1841-1872), English designer of bindings

Smith, Charles (fl.1830-1850), English binder

Smith, Charles Philip, 20th century English binder

Smith, Sally Lou (1925-   ), American binder in London

Solar, Josef, 20th century Czech binder

Solon, Léon V., 19th century designer of bindings

Sonntag, Carl (1884-1930), German binder

Sparre, Eva de (Comtesse) (1870- ?), Swedish binder

Staggemeier, L., 18-19th century binder in London

Stahly, Claude, 20th century French binding designer

Starr, Ellen Gates, 20th century American binder

Statlander, Fredrik W. (1756-1832), Swedish binder

Steel, Robert, 17th century English binder

Steel, Jane, 18th century English binder

Steinlen, Theophile A. (1859-1923), Swiss illustrator, lithographer, and
    designer of bindings in Paris

Stemmle, Josef, 20th century Swiss binder

Stikeman, Henry, 20th century American binder

Stroobants, J. (died 1922), French binder

Suarez, Antonio, 19th century Spanish binder

Sullivan, Edward (Sir) (1852-1928), English finisher

Sumner, Heywood (1853-1940), English etcher and designer of bindings

Sutcliffe, George (1878-1943), London binder

Swaim, William (fl.1805-17), American binder

Symon, Miroslava (1938-   ), Czech binder

Szántó, Tibor, 20th century Hungarian book designer for covers and
    jackets

Szirmai, John A. (1925-   ), Czech binder

Tegner, Hans (1853-1932), Danish painter, illustrator, and designer of
    bindings

Tessier, N. (fl.1780-1843?), French binder

Thevin, Santiago, 18th century Spanish binder

Thierry, 19-20th century French binder

Thiersch, Frieda (1889-1947), German binder

Thomas, Thomas, 16th century English printer and binder

Thomson, Hugh (1860-1920), Irish illustrator and designer of book covers

Thornton, Robert (fl.1692-1705), Irish binder

Thouvenin, Joseph (1790-1834), French binder

Tintore, Bartolomeo, 15th century Italian binder

Tochiori, Kumiko (1928–   ), Japanese binder

Traquair, Phoebe A. (1852–1936), Irish painter, decorator, and binder in Edinburgh

Trautz, Georges, 19th century German binder and gilder in Paris

Tribolet, Harold W., 20th century American binder

Vallgren, Antoinette, 19th century French binder

Varlin, Eugène (1839–1871), French binder

Vatter, Johannes (Dominican monk), Swiss Renaissance binder

Vecellio, Cesare (c.1530–1601), painter and decorator of bindings and fore-edges of Pillone bindings

Velde, Henry van de (1863–1957), Belgian architect, painter, engraver, designer, and creator of the German Jugendstil. Designed some bindings for books.

Vente, Pierre (fl.1765–1776), French binder

Verburg, Peter, 19–20th century American binder

Vermorel (died 1925), French binder and decorator

Vinding, Kirsten, 20th century French binding designer

Virin, Carl-Axel, 20th century Swedish binding designer

Vogel, E., 19th century German binder in Paris

Vogel, Friedrich W. (1816–1883), German binder in Jena

Vogt, Carl W. (1802–1879), Berlin binder

Volcker, Diedrich (died 1705 or 1706), Swedish binder

Wahlström, Hakan, 20th century Swedish binding designer

Walters, Curtis, 20th century American binder

Walther, Henry (1740s–1824?), German binder in London

Warren, Albert Henry (1830–1911), English designer of bindings

Waters, Peter, 20th century English binder

Wedel, Nils, 20th century Swedish binding designer

Weiersmuller, Peter (1944-   ), Swiss binder in Germany

Weil, Hope G., 20th century American binder, teacher, and collector

Weill, Lucie, 20th century French binder

Weiss, Emil R. (1875-1943), German painter, poet, type designer, and book designer

Weisse, Franz (1878-1952), German binder

Westwood, W. J. (1919-   ), English binder

Whitaker, John, 18th century English binder

White, Gleeson (1851-1898), English art writer and designer (including bindings)

Wiemeler, Ignatz (1895?-1952), German binder

Wiener, René (fl.1878-1893), French binder

Wier, Richard, 18th century English binder

Wilcox, Michael, 20th century Canadian binder

Wilhelmi, Johan T. (1713-1798), Danish binder

Willette, Adolphe L. (1857-1926), French painter, designer, writer, and designer of bindings

Wills, Francis M., 19th century Maryland binder

Wilson, James (1836-1916), Aberdeen bookseller and binder

Wirz, Verena (1945-   ), Swiss binder

Woolf, Leonard (1880-1969), English writer on politics and economics and binder

Woolf, Virginia (1882-1941), English novelist, critic, essayist, and binder

Wollenberg, Leah (1906-   ), American binder

Woltmann, Tider, 15th century German binder

Womersley, Edward P. (1909-   ), English binder

Wood, Harry (fl.1849-1893), English binder

Wright, John (fl.1835-1854), English binder

Ximénez, Felix, 18th century Spanish binder

Yardley, Harry J. Desmond (1905–1972), Irish binder in England

Youngers, Charles, 20th century American binder

Zach, Ferdinand, 20th century American binder

Zachrisson, Waldemar (1861–1924), Swedish printer and typographer who helped to revive interest in Swedish binding about 1885

Zaehnsdorf, Joseph (1816–1886), Austro-Hungarian binder in London

Zaehnsdorf, Joseph William (1853–1930), English binder and writer on binding

Zahn, Otto (1857–1928), German binder in Memphis, Tennessee

Zetti, Italo (1913–   ), wood engraver and binding decorator

Zoll, Johannes, 15th century German binder

BOOK COLLECTORS

Abbey, John Roland (Major), 20th century English collector

Alfonso V (1396-1458), King of Aragon (Spain) and Naples and a book
    collector

Beckford, William (1760-1844), English collector

Béraldi, Henri (1849-1931), French collector and iconographer

Davis, Henry (died Jan. 1977), British manufacturer and collector

Doucet, Jacques (1853-1929), French couturier, art patron, and book
    collector

Filareto, Apollonio, 16th century abbot, papal secretary, and book
    collector

Fürstenberg, Hans (1888 or 9?-   ), German banker and wit of his age.
    Changed name to Jean when he fled to France in 1933. Collected
    illustrated books and bindings of every period, but best known for
    French books of the 18th and early 19th century and his collection
    of German literature of the classical and pre-classical period.
    See article about him in Book collector 9:423-34, winter 1960.

Fugger family, 16th century German merchants and bankers to emperors and
    popes. Raimondo, John Jacob, Marcus, Ulrich, and Philip Edward were
    all book collectors.

Granvelle, Antoine Perrenot de (1517-1586), Spanish cardinal, statesman,
    and book collector. Born at Besançon, France.

Grimaldi, Giovanni Battista (1524?-c.1611), Genoese nobleman and book
    collector. See entry in Glaister's Glossary of the book (2d ed.,
    1979), p. 205.

Grolier, Jean (1479-1565), famous French bibliophile, especially of
    elegant bindings

Harley, Robert (1661-1724), 1st earl of Oxford. English statesman and
    founder of the famous Harleian collection

Mahieu (Maiolus), Thomas, 16th century French book collector

Marguerite de France (Marguerite de Valois) (1553-1615), wife of Henry IV
    of France and a great bibliophile. "It is now thought that [her
    collection] was made for Pietro Duodo, Venetian ambassador to France
    about 1600."--Glaister's Glossary of the book (2d ed., 1979)

Matthias I Corvinus (Mátyás Hunyadi) (1443-1490), King of Hungary from 1458 to 1490 and a book collector

Mendoza, Diego H. de (1503-1575), Spanish diplomat, scholar, poet, historian, and book collector. He formed his library while he was Spanish ambassador to Venice from 1540 to 1546. Nearly all his books were splendidly bound in one Venetian shop.

Morgan, John P. (1837-1913), American financier and book collector. His son, J. P. Morgan, Jr. (1867-1943) added to his father's collection and dedicated it to the public.

Papantonio, Michael, 20th century American book collector. Partner in firm of the Seven Gables Bookshop (as of 1972).

Pillone, Antonio, 16th century Italian book collector in Belluno

Pillone, Odorico (1503-1594), Italian jurist and book collector in Belluno

Poor, Henry William (1844-1915), American banker, expert in railroads, and book collector

Sickles, Daniel, 20th century American collector

Spencer, William A. (died 1912), a wealthy American who lived in Paris and accumulated a distinguished collection of 19th century bindings and illustrations, chiefly French. He willed his collection to the New York Public Library.

Thou, Jacques A. de (1553-1617), French statesman, historian, and bibliophile

Weiss, Giuseppe Weil (Baron) (1863-1939), binding collector

Wotton, Thomas (1521-1587), English patron of learning and a bibliophile

GLOSSARY

A petit fers. A French term used to describe tooling a design with small individual tools.

Artiste-relieur. French term for binding designer.

Blind tooling. Impressions on the cover of a book made by tools or dies without the use of ink or leaf.

Bosses. Brass or other metal ornamentations fastened upon the boards of books.

Cameo binding. A binding decorated with a cameo stamp.

Cartonnage. Simple cased-in board binding.

Centro del Bel Libro. A workshop in Ascona, Switzerland for handmade paper and bindings.

Champlevé enamel bindings. The enameling is done by engraving out the solid surface so as to leave little pools or hollows which are to be filled with enamel.

Cloisonné enamel bindings. The enameling is done by building up upon the metal surface very small partitions, dividing up the field into little compartments.

Club Bindery. Started in 1895 by some of the members of the Grolier Club in New York City.

Cosway bindings. Bindings produced by Rivière in the early years of the 20th century. Miss Currie, who may have been influenced by Richard Cosway, English miniaturist (1740-1821), did the ivory miniatures. Cosway was a master in the use of materials, including ivory.

Cottage binding. "A decorative binding in which the centre panel was often given a gable at head and foot, and the spaces filled with a variety of interlacings, sprays, and small tools. Although this style may have originated in France, it is most characteristic of English bindings of the late 17th century to 1710."--Harrod's Librarians' glossary, 3rd ed., 1971.

Cuir ciselé bindings. See Lederschnittbände.

Dentelle binding. A binding having a border with a lacy pattern on the inner edge. Notable binders in this style were the Derôme family and Pierre-Paul Dubuisson.

Designer Bookbinders. The new name (as of 1968) of the Guild of Contemporary binders. The group is composed of English craft binders.

Doreur. French term for gilder.

Doreur sur cuir. French term for a gilder of leather or finisher.

Doublure. Decorative linings of watered silk, vellum or tooled leather fitted to the inside face of the boards of a handbound book.

Doves Bindery. A bindery set up in 1893 by Thomas J. Cobden-Sanderson in Hammersmith, London.

Edition binding. The uniform binding of large quantities of single titles or sets of books.

Embossed binding. A binding with a design or designs in relief.

Entrelacs. Interlacing ribbons or strapwork.

Etruscan binding. A calfskin binding decorated with patterns adopted from Etruscan vases and other classical ornaments. William Edwards of Halifax used the style in the 18th century.

Ex-libris. A mark of ownership of books.

Fanfare. "A style of book cover decoration developed and practiced in France from about 1570 to 1640. The main features are interlacing ribbons forming compartments of various shapes, with emphasis given to a central compartment. This interlacing ribbon is bounded by a double line on one side and a single line on the other. As fully developed naturalistic floral and foliage ornaments, made with small hand tools, often azured, fill all the compartments except the central one and almost completely cover the sides."--Glaister's Glossary of the book, 2d ed., 1979.

Finishing. A term for the completion of binding after the book has been put into its case, such as polishing, ornamenting, lettering, and pressing.

Forwarding. In hand leather binding the term means inserting plates, sewing, tying into boards, and covering with leather. In edition binding the word means all the processes between the folding of the sheets and putting the book into its cover.

Gardes, pages de gardes. French term for fly leaf; in a bound work, endpaper.

Goffered edges (or gauffered edges or chased edges). The gilt edges of a book with indentions.

Guild of Book Workers. A national organization that is affiliated with the American Institute of Graphic Arts.

Guild of Contemporary Binders. See Designer Bookbinders.

Guild of Women-Binders. An association of English women binders formed in 1898 by Frank Karslake. The group was associated with the Hampstead Bindery.

Hampstead Bindery. A workshop of English craftsmen binders established around 1900.

Harleian bindings. Bindings made by Thomas Elliott and Christopher Chapman for Robert Harley, 1st Earl of Oxford (1661-1724). Most of them are in red morocco with an ornate center-piece and a broad border, or a narrow roll border.

Lederschnittbände. German name for bindings made in the cuir ciselé (cut leather) manner. They are made of thick dark leather and ornamented with plant or animal forms. Germany and Austria produced them in the 15th century.

Mosaic binding. Bindings with inlaid designs.

Mudéjar binding. Spanish strapwork binding made by Moorish binders.

Plaquette binding. A binding with medallions in the center of the cover as the main decoration.

Pointillé binding. "Gold-tooled decoration on leather binding producing a dotted effect, whether by the repetition of single dots or by the use of tools with dotted instead of solid outlines."--Howard M. Nixon.

Relievo leather binding. Practiced particularly by the firm of Remnant and Edmonds. See Private library 7:129-30, autumn 1974.

Relieur. French term for craftsman binder.

Reliure originale. French term for art binding as opposed to a publisher's binding.

Reliures vernis sans odeur. A group of lacquered bindings made in Paris in the early part of the 19th century. Theodore Pierre Bertin made a number of them. Simon-Etienne Martin made the translucent lacquer and secured a patent for it in 1730.

Roll. A binder's revolving tool used for running lines or designs on a book cover. Also called a fillet or a roulette. In French, filet or is gold fillet, and filet à froid is fillet in blind.

Rowfant Club. A club established in 1895 for bibliophiles in Cleveland, Ohio.

Roxburghe binding. A style of binding used for the Roxburghe Club formed in London in 1812.

Roycroft Press. A private press and bindery founded in 1893 by Elbert Hubbard (1856-1915) at East Aurora, N. Y.

Société de la Reliure Originale. A group formed in 1945 of French art binders.

Super-exlibris. A panel stamp in center of front cover to indicate
    ownership. Also known as supralibros.

Tooling, The impressing of designs into a leather or cloth binding.

Tools. Hand stamps and tools used in finishing.

Vernis martins. See Reliures vernis sans odeur.

AUTHOR INDEX

The numbers in this index refer to entry numbers, not page numbers.

Garvey, Eleanor M., 650

Gasiorowska, Maria J., 381, 1112

Gaskell, Philip, 403

Gaskill and Copper, firm, Phila., 168

Gauffecourt, Jean-Vincent Capronnier de, 72

Gauthier, Marie-Madeleine, 564, 565

Geck, E., 685

Geldner, Ferdinand, 299, 686, 687

Gelli, Jacopo, 1425

Gerlach, Martin, 187, 326

Ghosh, A., 994

Giannini, Giulio G., 81

Gibson, Strickland, 811, 812

Gibstone, J. C., 939

Gid, D., 1343

Gimpel & Weitzenhoffer, N.Y., 1276

Girard, Henri, 617

Giraud, Jean B., 618

Glaister, Geoffrey A., 20

Glauning, Otto, 732

Gnoli, Tommaso, 1019

Godenne, Willy, 463, 1077

Göpel, Erhard, 733

Goff, Frederick R., 688, 1234

Goldschmidt, Ernst P., 116, 364, 382, 383

Goldschmidt, Werner, 1141

Goodhue, Bertram G., 1452

Goodman, Philip, 1427-31

Gore, Gary, 1515

Gorenflo, Edward, firm, 95

Graham, Rigby, 160, 1066

Grand-Carteret, John, 543

Gratzl, Emil, 996, 1005, 1106

Grautoff, Otto, 721, 722, 734

Gray, George J., 813

Great Britain. Arts Council, 651

Greene, Douglas G., 1252

Greeven, E. A., 735

Griesbach, Elsie, 544

Grieve, Alastair, 888

Grimm, Verna B., 1376

Grimsditch, Herbert B., 1506

Grohmann, Adolf, 503

Grolier Club, N.Y., 4, 130, 206, 268, 287, 384, 1235, 1277

Grover, Rachel, 176

Gruel, Léon, 5, 229, 518, 545, 566, 619-21

Guégan, Bertrand, 212

Guiffrey, J. J., 596

Guigard, Joannis, 1404

Guignard, Jacques, 670

Guild of Women Binders, London, 889

Gullans, Charles B., 1278

Gulyás, Paul, 980

Gumachian & Cie, 288

Gwynn, Frederick L., 936

SUBJECT INDEX

The numbers in this index refer to entry numbers, not page numbers.

Bookplates, 1373-71; reference
works, 1384, 1387, 1390, 1391,
1393, 1394, 1399; art and technique, 1400-03; armorial, 1383,
1385, 1404, 1407, 1439; artists
and designers, 1375, 1382, 1394,
1398, 1402; French, 1410; Great
Britain, 1417, 1420; Netherlands,
1435; United States, 1448, 1450,
1451, 1455; Children, 1397;
ladies', 1392; military, 1388;
miniature, 1389; owners, 1382;
study of, 1465-71; Belgium, 1436;
Great Britain, 1417-24; France,
1404-10; Germany, 1411-16; Italy,
1425, 1426; Japan, 1463; Jewish,
1427-32; Netherlands, 1433-36;
Portugal, 1439, 1440; Russia,
1441-44; Spain, 1445, 1446;
Sweden, 1461; Spanish America,
1464; United States, 1447-60;
Delaware, 1454; Pennsylvania
Germans, 1449

Boyer (or Boyet), 581

Bozérian, Jean Claude, 612

Brabant, Belgium: bookbinding, 471

Brazil: book jackets, 1526

Brugalla, Emilio, 1167, 1168

Brugalla, Santiago, 1167

Buglass, Caleb, 1230

Bulkley, M. E., 1245

Burn, James and Co., 879

Byzantine binding, 354

Cambridge, England: binders, 813

Cameo bookstamps, 839

Canapé, 607, 623, 631

Canevari, Demetrio, 1036. See
also Canevari bindings, Giovanni
Grimaldi

Canevari bindings, 1027, 1028, 1034,
1036, 1039, 1054. See also
Hungary, Giovanni Grimaldi

Care and repair of bindings, 330,
1307-37; bibliography, 1307-11;
general works, 1312-26; leather
and parchment, 1327-37

Carolingian bookbindings, 349, 350,
356

Carsi y Vidal, Pascual, 1157, 1158

Cartonnages: French mosaic, 608;
19th century France, 622, 629

Cataloging of bindings, 330

Caumont, Auguste Marie de (Comte),
890

Caxton, William, 823

Chapin, Elizabeth G., 1245

Charrière, Gérard, 1276, 1289

China: care and repair of bindings,
473; history, 472, 474; technique of binding, 474

Church luxury volumes: medieval,
367, 368, 374. See also mass
books

Clarke, John, 891

Clements, Henry John B.: collection of armorial bindings, 783

Clements, Jeff, 948

Cloth bindings: classification and
description, 105, 107, 1352, 1355,
1356; history, 100, 101, 103, 104;
Great Britain, 870; United States,
1259

Club Bindery, New York City, 1245,
1277, 1293, 1294

Cobden-Sanderson, Thomas J., 407,
872, 873, 874, 905, 909, 919

Cockerell, Sydney Morris, 950

About the Compiler

VITO J. BRENNI, Ph.D., has taught at Duquesne University and the State University of New York. His earlier books include *American English: A Bibliogaphy*, *William Dean Howells: A Bibliography*, *Essays in Bibliography*, and *Book Illustration and Decoration: A Guide to Research* (Greenwood Press, 1980).